D1220722

FILM and the DIRECTOR

THE MACMILLAN COMPANY
NEW YORK · CHICAGO
DALLAS · ATLANTA · SAN FRANCISCO
LONDON · MANILA

IN CANADA
BRETT-MACMILLAN LTD.
GALT, ONTARIO

FILM
and the
DIRECTOR

by

DON LIVINGSTON

The Macmillan Company
New York

PRINTED IN THE UNITED STATES OF AMERICA

Fourth Printing, 1960

TO BETTY

INTRODUCTION

The abilities of the good film director result from experiences and talents impossible to transmit. No book can teach a person to direct motion pictures; it can only explain basic principles and outline some of the problems. That is the purpose of this book.

The motion picture director is involved in almost all of the varied and complex phases of film production. He is the man who coordinates all the efforts which translate the written scenario into the visual images and audible effects of the finished film. These efforts involve many different craftsmen and technicians: cameramen, set designers, writers, business men, electricians, actors, make-up artists, film editors, sound engineers, and many others. All of these specialists contribute to the making of a film, and the director must understand the basic principles of each of their crafts. And yet, all too often, the specialists themselves know surprisingly little about the work of the director or about the work of the other specialists. In this book I hope to acquaint technicians with the work of the director and of other technicians, to contribute to a greater unity of effort, and thus make the job of the director less difficult.

Motion pictures—their production, distribution, and presentation

—are today in one of the most critical phases of their turbulent history. As a result of competition from television, many theaters are closing, and the industry is desperately searching for a way to revive a deflated box office. Drive-in theaters, Cinerama, Cinema-Scope, and three-dimensional films are attempts in this direction. Just what the outcome will be is difficult to predict. However, one fact is becoming increasingly evident. While distribution and presentation may suffer retrenchment and undergo radical changes in the next few years, the production of films eventually will expand far beyond its present capacities. Television, now turning from the live show to the more easily handled film presentation, will consume many times as much film as the theater. Directing these films for television is sometimes more complex than directing theatrical features. The extremely limited budgets for television allow no tolerance for guesswork.

From the creative viewpoint, it makes little difference whether the film is destined for the theater or the television screen. Wide screen and three-dimensional processes may prevent such films being shown on television, and there may be minor differences in techniques among the different film forms. Basic production principles, however, will remain relatively unchanged, and the talents and abilities necessary to produce one form will also be required in the production of other film forms.

It is my hope that the thoughts expressed in this book will help in the uncovering of those talents and the development of those abilities which will be needed in a greatly expanded industry.

August 1953   Don Livingston

CONTENTS

FILM and the DIRECTOR

CHAPTER ONE

THE SCREEN TECHNIQUE

When time began, man's sense of sight was probably much the same as it is today. His speech, however, and his communication to his fellows were limited to a few grunts of varying tones and amplitude and a warning grimace to keep others from his food and his mate. Slowly, with the passing of centuries, his grunts and grimaces developed into speech, and man communicated his ideas and thoughts by means of the spoken word.

However, the use of the spoken word was limited to direct communication and was soon found to be unsatisfactory for many purposes. Man could make no record of his thoughts, nor could he send messages without the use of the word-of-mouth messenger. Thus, he started to draw crude pictures on the walls of his cave or on large, flat pieces of stone. These pictures—crude, still, and lifeless—were to form the basis of two definite forms of communication.

On the one hand, the pictures became simplified into symbols and from symbols, into letters and words. On the other hand, the crude pictures were developed into more lifelike representations and with the invention of oils, into the great paintings which form so important a part of our artistic heritage.

1

With these developments in the communication of ideas and thoughts, man also developed his appreciation and understanding. As patterns evolved in the use of the written and spoken word, the mind became trained to think according to these patterns. Certain word formations produced certain mental images, and writers and speakers became known for their styles, styles which they found were conducive to desired psychological receptions. The same was true with painting. Artists found that their composition and colors could have a striking influence upon the onlooker. Today, different schools of artists are experimenting with entirely new psychological approaches, variously labeled "modern" and "impressionistic." In spite of the long and continuing development of civilized communication and thinking, however, man today still associates those things which he sees about him much the same as he did ages ago.

We understand what we see because we see it in its entirety. We are limited only by the horizon and by our ability to turn our head and eyes. If we are standing by the side of the road and see an approaching car, we can turn our eyes and head to watch it as it comes near, passes us, and finally disappears over the distant hill. Or, if we wish, we can take our eyes from the car to look at a farmhouse across the road, and from the farmhouse we can shift our eyes to the cattle in the near-by field. However, as we shift our gaze from one object to another, we see everything in between. Our world of sight knows no limits, and we can turn from one thing to another, understanding them because of our consciousness of the landscape between objects. We see everything in complete relationship to everything else, and thus we understand any setting we are in. All our waking hours are filled with sight, and it is only when we awaken in a strange setting that our sight confuses us. It was this way with the earliest man as he was struggling to develop speech, and it is this way with us today.

Consider, however, the limits of the motion picture or television screen. It is bound rigidly on four sides, and we know nothing of the setting except that which is within those set boundaries.

If the cameraman who took the scene were to shift his camera as quickly as we do our eyes, the result on the screen would be an unrecognizable blur, not the normal shift from object to object we get when we shift our eyes. Too, if a different scene flashed on the screen we would be as lost as if we suddenly awoke in a strange place. Somehow this new scene must be explained, or we must watch it long enough to be able to study it and understand its meaning. How, then, with all these limitations can the screen condense the happenings of a year or two—or even a lifetime—into a few short reels of film? Since we have been trained from the earliest beginnings of man to accept anything we see in relationship to everything else we see, how can the screen delete all these relationships and condense the happenings of days into minutes, hours into seconds? The answer is by substituting a whole new set of visual experiences which are closely enough related to man's normal seeing experiences so that he will understand and accept what he sees on the screen. These new visual experiences have resulted from the screen techniques upon which the creation of a motion picture or television presentation is based. These techniques are the tricks which, properly used, give us pictorial continuity. Improperly used, they will only confuse and mislead.

Screen techniques, which are the stock in trade of the screen director, fall generally into two classes. First, we have those which join scenes or pieces of film. Secondly, we have those which shift attention within a scene or piece of film. A motion picture is simply a succession of scenes which probably were not photographed in the order in which we see them. Rather they were shot according to the availability of sets, locations, and the contracting of the actors. Photographing them so that they will fit together to tell a story is one of the major problems of the screen director.

JOINING SCENES

The most generally used method of joining scenes is the *cut*. A cut is simply an instantaneous change of scene. If we take two pieces of film, splice them together, and show the result on the screen, we will see a cut. It may be a good cut, or it may be a bad cut. It may add to our understanding, or it may confuse us. Its proper use is the basis of the motion picture technique, and it must be understood by all who would understand how ideas are translated on the moving screen.

Another method of joining scenes is the *optical*. Opticals are so called because they are made "optically" on the motion picture printer. One type is the *fade*. In the fade, the screen becomes gradually darker until the entire frame is black, or vice versa, the screen starts black and grows lighter until the complete scene is visible. The first type, in which the scene disappears, is called the *fade-out*. The second type, in which the scene appears from blackness, is called the *fade-in*. Fades may be long or short, slow or fast, depending on the tempo of the sequence. A fade-in is usually used at the beginning of a film, and a fade-out at the end. They also are used in pairs within the film to mark major divisions, not unlike the chapters in a book. In the minds of the audience, the fade establishes a passage of time and perhaps a shift in locale.

Closely allied to the fade is another optical, the *dissolve*. In the dissolve, one scene gradually melts into another. Like fades, they can be long or short, slow or fast, depending on the tempo desired. The effect of the dissolve upon the audience is somewhat like the fade except that the shift in time or locale is not so drastic. The fade is often a drastic shift in both time and locale, while the dissolve often marks a shift of locale with only a minor passage of time. The dissolve marks a change not unlike that from one paragraph to another.

Not so generally used, but appearing in certain types of films, is another type of optical called the *wipe*. The wipe is a transition in which one scene is rubbed off simultaneously with the appearance of another scene. The effect is as if an invisible roller passes across the screen and wipes out one scene as the next is revealed. In a wipe the displacement takes place through optical movement; in a dissolve it takes place through superimposure.

Opticals are generally used to mark the division between sequences.* Cuts mark the division between scenes † within a sequence. Movement is used to shift attention within a scene.

TRANSITION BY MOVEMENT

By the use of movement, the film-maker can lead the eyes of the audience from one thing to another and offer many interesting transitions. Generally, movement falls into two classes: subject movement and camera movement. The first, of course, is simply the movement of the person or object being photographed, and the second is the movement of the camera photographing the scene.

There are several types of *camera movement*. Probably the most used is the *pan*, a simple horizontal turning of the camera from a fixed point. The effect of the pan on the screen is much the same as when we slowly turn our eyes to look over a landscape or follow a moving object.

The *tilt*, similar to the pan, is the vertical movement of the camera from a fixed point. The effect of the tilt on the screen is that of moving our eyes up or down.

The *truck* or *dolly shot* results from actually moving the entire camera. This is accomplished by mounting the camera on a wagon-like affair known as a *dolly*, placing the dolly on preset tracks, and pushing it to and fro as desired.

The following examples might clarify the different classes of movement.

SUBJECT MOVEMENT

The scene is the front of a farmhouse. Leading from the front porch is a brick walk. It follows a winding path, so as to avoid several trees, down toward the road which is our vantage point. An ancient farmer is sitting on an old-fashioned rocker on

* See definition of sequence, p. 12.
† See definition of scene, p. 12.

An Example of
SUBJECT
MOVEMENT

Farmer walks from
LONG-SHOT farmer
into **CLOSE-UP** farmer

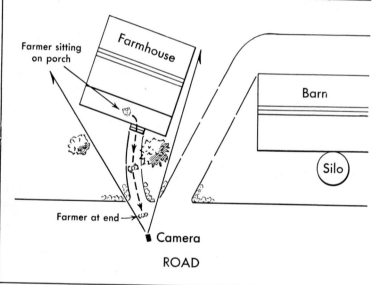

Farmer sitting on porch

Farmhouse

Barn

Silo

Farmer at end

Camera

ROAD

An Example of
CAMERA MOVEMENT

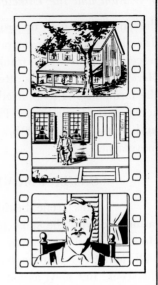

CAMERA DOLLIES from
LONG-SHOT farmer
to **CLOSE-UP** farmer

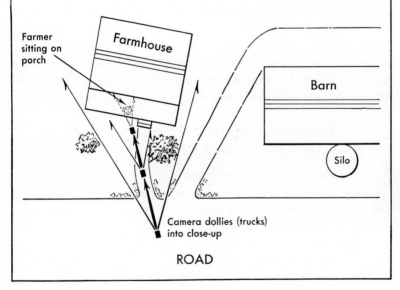

Farmer sitting on porch

Farmhouse

Barn

Silo

Camera dollies (trucks) into close-up

ROAD

the porch. He gets up from the chair and comes up the walk, directly toward the camera. He becomes larger and larger in the screen until the whole frame is filled with his head and shoulders. Here he stops, in sharp, attention-getting focus. In the background, the farmhouse is so blurred and indistinct that it is no longer an active part of our scene. The transition from *long shot* * to *close-up* † of the farmer has been accomplished solely through subject movement.

CAMERA MOVEMENT

This scene begins as did the previous one, the same farmhouse with the same farmer sitting on the same front porch. He is so small in relation to the house and the front lawn with walk and trees that he hardly registers on the mind as part of the scene. But now, as we watch, the camera slowly moves closer to the house. Our screen is filled with the porch; then it narrows to the front door and, beside it, the farmer on the chair. The camera moves still closer until the head and shoulders of the farmer fill the frame. Again, our transition has been from long shot to close-up of the farmer, but this time we have accomplished it through camera movement—a dolly shot.

COMBINED SUBJECT
AND CAMERA MOVEMENT

Once more our scene starts as did the other two. We see the same farmhouse with the farmer on the porch. As we watch, he gets up from the chair, walks part way up the walk, and then turns to walk diagonally across the lawn. In order to keep him in the frame, the camera pans to the right, and we see new objects and terrain. In the background is a large red barn, and leading from it, toward the camera, is a well-used dirt road. Coming from the barn is a tractor, driven by a tow-headed youngster of sixteen. The

* See definition of long shot, p. 17.
† See definition of close-up, p. 17.

An Example of
COMBINED MOVEMENT

Farmer walks from porch toward **CAMERA** — then he turns toward barn. **CAMERA PANS** revealing boy on tractor. Farmer walks out of scene as boy moves into **CLOSE-UP**.

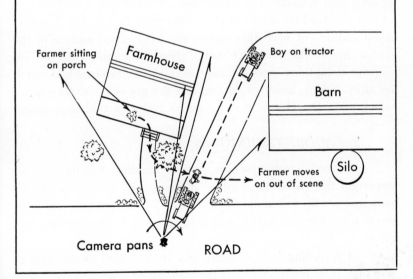

Farmer sitting on porch

Farmhouse

Boy on tractor

Barn

Silo

Farmer moves on out of scene

Camera pans

ROAD

farmer crosses the road in front of the tractor and continues on out of the scene. The camera, as if finding a new interest, holds on the tractor and boy until they have approached so close that the boy is now in a head-and-shoulder close-up. In this one scene, the attention was shifted from the farmhouse, to the farmer, to the barn with the approaching tractor, to a close-up of the boy. Combined subject and camera movement was the visual tool.

COMBINED VISUAL TECHNIQUES

Frequently, in the better films, we will see subject movement and all the various camera movements, pan, tilt, and dolly, combined into one smoothly executed, well-planned scene. It is in this way that the director gets fluidity and flow, and consequent interest, into his film. Movement, the cut, and the opticals are the basic tools of visual technique, and with their proper use, the director can translate the happenings of days into a reel or two of film and lead the minds of the audience so that they will understand and accept what they see on the flat, limited surface of the screen. Before the advent of sound, these techniques, plus the use of printed captions, were the only methods the director had to tell his story. Today, however, he can add the use of audio techniques which make the film to most people as real as actual happenings.

AUDIO TECHNIQUES

Audio techniques are four in number, and they are so important that the well-organized studio usually has a separate department set up to handle the technical aspects of each. They are direct recording, narration—including lip sync,* sound effects, and music.

Direct recording is that sound actually recorded at the time of shooting. It, of course, includes the dialogue or speech of the actors. On the finished film it is supported by sound effects, music, and sometimes narration. Narration is the running commentary by an unseen speaker which often accompanies certain types of films. Sound effects, as the name implies, are those sounds which could

* See definition of lip sync, p. 113.

not or were not recorded at the time of shooting and are therefore added to the film during the final phases of production after shooting has been completed. Background music, which heightens the emotional effect, is also added during the final phases of production.

TYPES OF FILMS

Films may be generally classified as to newsreel or continuity type, depending upon the use they make of the various visual and audio techniques.

The newsreel-type film is usually compiled and edited from large quantities of scenes and limited sequences which received little or no direction during their production. Lacking, therefore, the stress on visual techniques during their production, these scenes must depend upon narration to give meaning, even after they are edited and appear as a completed picture. Without explanatory narration, newsreel-type films carry little or no meaning to the audience.

The continuity-type film is carefully planned, pictorially, before a camera is turned, and therefore it makes full use of the visual techniques which carry most messages far better than mere words. A good continuity film will often carry a great portion of its message even if the sound is turned off.

Frequently, one motion picture makes use of both methods of presentation. With points or aspects of the message which need amplification, the continuity technique is used; with related points which need not be covered so fully, the newsreel technique is used. Documentaries, short subjects, and training films are motion pictures of this nature. Sometimes, even in theatrical feature films, which are largely of the continuity type, the newsreel technique will be used to condense time and material.

THE SHOT, THE SCENE, AND THE SEQUENCE

The dictionary defines a scene as one of the divisions of a drama during which there is no change of place nor lapse in continuity of time. This definition is generally accepted in story-construction and in viewing completed films or plays. However, in shooting and cutting together the individual pieces of film which make up a motion picture, we must not only define the dramatic divisions, but we must define the individual pieces of film which make up those divisions. Furthermore, we must define the different compositions or picture images in the individual pieces of film, for movement may cause a single piece of film to have any number of variations of long shot to close-up and back again.

As a result of these and other complications, the film industry is beset with a conflict of terminology. Both the terms *scene* and *shot* are used to denote a single piece of film. The word *shot* is also used to denote any given composition. Furthermore, because a motion picture can jump quickly from place to place and is not tied as closely to physical limits as is the stage drama, the word, *scene,* and a new word, *sequence,* are often used to refer to any dramatic division.

Various writers and authorities have tried, without success, to standardize the meanings of these terms. It is not my purpose to add further to this confusion, but in order to discuss matters intelligently we must arrive at a common use of terms.

In our discussion of the screen technique, *we may think of a scene as a single piece of film in which there is neither a cut nor an optical.*

A shot may be defined as any given composition within a scene. In the previous example of subject movement, the scene began with a long shot and ended with a close-up. Thus, this scene, or piece of film, had several shots. In many cases, however, where there is no movement and the composition does not change, a scene and a shot are practically synonymous.

A sequence is a unit of continuous action in which there is no lapse of time. A sequence may be, but is not necessarily, tied to the limit of place. For example: after an optical, we see a boy and a girl enter a drugstore. They order milk-shakes from the young chap behind the counter and engage in conversation with the elderly druggist. After the milk-shakes are prepared, the druggist goes about his business in another part of the store, and the boy and girl enjoy their drinks. As they leave the counter, the girl enters a phone booth and calls her mother. As the conversation takes place, we see, alternately, the mother at the phone in her home and the girl at the phone in the drugstore. When the conversation is over, the girl moves out of the phone booth, rejoins the boy, and together they leave the store. After an optical, our next scene is a long shot of a race track.

The unit of continuous action in the drugstore and in the mother's home constitutes a sequence.

The sequence is the basis of the continuity-type film. It may be composed of many scenes, or in some cases it may be only a single scene. Its proper relationship to the film as a whole and the proper interrelationship of the scenes which compose it are vital to the organization of the continuity film.

ORGANIZATION OF THE CONTINUITY FILM

The continuity film, the type with which the director is most often concerned, is composed of half a dozen or more *sequences.*

Each sequence is usually separated from the remainder of the film by *opticals.*

Within the individual sequences, the different scenes are joined together by means of the *cut.*

Within each scene, transitions are secured by means of *movement.*

The most important aspect of the screen technique is the proper execution of the cut and of movement. The proper execution of the cut causes the audience to think of the sequence as one continuous piece of film, and the proof of good cutting is its failure to attract the attention of the audience. *Proper* movement lends the film grace, depth, interest, and pace, and with its use we get a decrease in the number of cuts and a simultaneous increase in the number of photographic angles.

OUTLINE OF SCREEN TECHNIQUES

There are two general types of films:

1. Continuity-type films
2. Newsreel-type films

The *visual units* of a continuity-type film are:

1. Sequences
2. Scenes
3. Shots

The *transitions* which separate the visual units are:

1. Opticals
2. Cuts
3. Movements

The major *opticals* are:

1. Dissolves
2. Fades

Movements are of three classes:

1. Subject movement
2. Camera movement
3. Combined subject and camera movement

Camera movements are of three types:

1. Pan
2. Tilt
3. Truck (dolly)

There are four *audio techniques*:

1. Direct recording
2. Narration
3. Sound effects
4. Background music

An understanding of these terms and techniques and their inter-relationships is necessary to all film workers.

CHAPTER TWO

THE CUT

A basic knowledge of the mechanics of continuity cutting is essential to all who would work in the creative end of motion picture production. The writer must have at least a grasp of the fundamentals if he is to write credible scenarios and understand the other members of the production team. The cameraman, if he is to be of constructive help to the director, must know that problems of cutting do exist, and that no scene, however well photographed or beautiful the composition, is of use unless it can be cut smoothly with the rest of the scenes photographed. The editor is the specialist in this phase of screen ability, and to him cutting must be second nature. The director, however, must be able to visualize and stage his scenes in proper editorial terms; he must, upon demand, be able to look at the happenings about him in terms of angles and cuts, and those who would understand him should have at least an acquaintance with this basic technique of picture continuity.

How often have the director and the editor looked at each other helplessly because of the obstinacy of a writer or producer who does not understand the mechanical limitations of the cut? How many cameramen have felt personally insulted because the director could not take their well-meant suggestion for a striking piece of composition and lighting which, however well done, could only have landed on the cutting room floor? How many editors in the privacy of their cutting rooms have roundly berated a director because a sequence would not go together properly? How many pictures have been ruined because of poor cutting? Yes, those who would understand the creative end of motion picture production must first understand the mechanics of continuity cutting. They must realize that in the making of motion pictures, just as in all creative endeavors, mechanical rules of craftsmanship must first be learned before art can be applied.

ADVANTAGES OF THE CUT

The use of the cut gives the motion picture director an advantage never enjoyed by his stage counterpart. The stage is limited to one perspective, one viewpoint; the audience is always the same distance from the actors. On film, however, we can place the camera far back from the action and show—let us say—the entire action of a battlefield. Then, instantly, we can cut to a close shot of the soldiers as they move forward in the attack. We can follow this with a close shot of the enemy machine-gunners as they desperately fire their machine gun. Again we can cut back to a long shot of the battle and show the relationship of the two. By varying the angle and size of the scene, we can guide the attention of the audience and show them just what we choose: no more, no less. In a close shot of a soldier we can show the fear on his face, the wild look in his eye. Then, cutting to a longer shot, we can show the exploding shells and the devastation which cause the fear. Each scene bears a relationship to the one before it and the one after it. Our scope is unlimited, our control of the audience absolute.

However, in order to accomplish all this, we must follow certain mechanical rules in our cuts. By following them, we guide the audience into any desired channel of thought. By disregarding them, we confuse the audience and detract from the dramatic value of the film.

TYPES OF SHOTS

In order to discuss the mechanical rules of cutting, it is necessary that we understand the meanings of the terms *long shot, medium shot, close-up,* and *insert.* These terms refer to the amount of area included in a given shot.

A *long shot* includes considerable area around the subject, and the camera is usually some distance away.

A *close-up* includes only the subject, and the camera is usually quite close. If the subject is a person, a close-up includes only the head and shoulders.

A *medium shot,* as the name implies, is a shot intermediate between a long shot and a close-up.

An *insert* is merely an extreme close-up, usually of a person's hand or of an inanimate object.

In using these terms, it is important to be specific concerning the subject or object being featured. Just the term *long shot*—or *close-up*—is not sufficient. A close-up of a theater entrance, for example, might be a long shot of a person coming out of the theater.

Other terms which may be encountered are *medium long shot, medium close-up, full shot, two shot,* and *close shot.* These terms are merely relative and often have various shades of meaning, depending upon the thinking of the person who uses them. Generally, they will be avoided in our discussion of continuity cutting.

TYPES OF CONTINUITY CUTS

Continuity cuts are of two types: the *match cut* and the *cut-away.* A variation of the cut-away is the *cutback.* These labels refer to the relationship of the two shots, one on each side of the cut, which are being joined. *If the second of the two shots involved takes in a portion of the previous shot we have a match cut. If the second shot does not take in a portion of the previous shot, it is a cut-away.* A cutback is a form of cut-away in which we return to a scene shown just previously.

A short, silent sequence, with the types of cuts indicated, may clarify the differences.

1. EXTERIOR-DAY
   LONG SHOT
   CITY STREET
   The camera is shooting up the sidewalk as strolling pedestrians pass to and fro. John Lattimore approaches from the distance, and as he comes into a full figure shot, he is attracted by something in a jewelry store window. He stops, and then he walks over to the window, CAMERA PANNING WITH HIM.

2. EXTERIOR-DAY
   CLOSE-UP
   JOHN
   As he looks down into the window, he is thoughtful.

   A Match Cut
   John was in Scene 1.
   Scene 2 is merely a closer angle of him.

3. EXTERIOR TO INTERIOR-DAY
   INSERT
   THREE ENGAGEMENT RINGS IN WINDOW
   They are priced at $200, $298, and $499.

   A Cut-Away
   Scene 3 follows naturally after Scene 2. The camera sees what John is looking at. However, we could not see the rings in Scene 2.

4. EXTERIOR-DAY
   CLOSE-UP
   JOHN'S FACE
   He is thoughtful, almost wistful. Suddenly he becomes aware of someone approach-

   A Cut-Away (Also a *Cutback*)
   Scene 4 is merely a closer angle of John than in Scene 2; thus it is a cutback. With reference to Scene 3, it is a cut-away.

ing, and he turns away from camera.

5. EXTERIOR-DAY
   MEDIUM SHOT
   FRONT OF JEWELRY STORE
   John turns away from window as Mary Owens enters scene. She greets John.

A Match Cut
John is visible in both Scenes 4 and 5.

6. EXTERIOR-DAY
   MEDIUM TWO SHOT
   JOHN AND MARY
   They talk.

A Match Cut

7. EXTERIOR-DAY
   CLOSE-UP
   MARY
   She smiles at John.

A Match Cut

8. EXTERIOR-DAY
   CLOSE-UP
   JOHN
   He glances down at the rings, then at Mary.

A Cut-Away
In Scene 7 we could not see John.

9. EXTERIOR-DAY
   MEDIUM TWO SHOT
   JOHN AND MARY
   Angle is past John and favoring Mary. She, too, looks down at the rings, then at John. Her eyes twinkle, but she looks away as if to say, "No." She takes his arm, and they exit scene.

A Match Cut

THE MATCH CUT

The object of the match cut is to gain a continuity of action and idea which will keep the audience unaware of the change in scene. In so doing, an entire sequence, composed of many scenes, may appear to the audience like one continuous scene or piece of film. In order to accomplish this, the audience must see no difference in the position, dress, or expression of the actor at the instant of the cut. In other words, the second of the two scenes must "match" the first. If John was wearing an overcoat in Scene 1, he must wear an overcoat in Scene 2. If the overcoat collar is turned up in Scene 1, it must be turned up in Scene 2. If Mary was holding her pocketbook in her right hand in Scene 6, she must hold it in the same hand in Scene 7. The old-time movie in which the heroine emerged perfectly dry from the lake is an example of what may happen when this principle is not followed. In our foregoing sample sequence, John's overcoat would magically appear and disappear, and Mary's pocketbook would jump, most mysteriously, from hand to hand.

The study of matching action can become as complicated as the picture or imagination of the director. Basically, however, there are but three ways in which scenes must match. These are position, movement, and look.

MATCHING THE POSITION

We know that we cannot cut from a medium shot of a man in an overcoat to a close-up of him without the overcoat. Therefore, when shooting two scenes which are to be cut together, the director must be sure that each subject is dressed exactly the same in one scene as in the other. Furthermore, at the time the cut takes place, the physical position of the body must be the same. If the chin was resting on the hand at the end of one scene, it must be doing the same at the beginning of the next. This is called matching the position.

MATCHING THE MOVEMENT

People in an audience see just a flat screen bound on four sides; they see only what the camera shows them. Now, if they should see a man walking from left to right across the screen, and

MATCHING the MOVEMENT

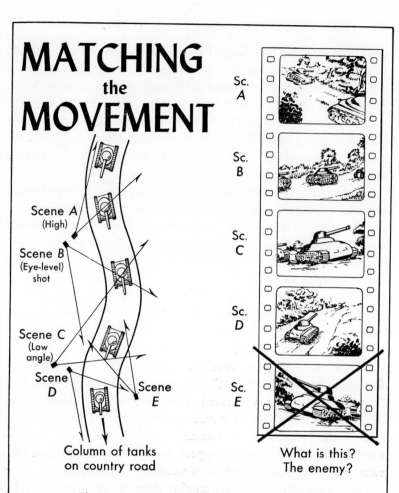

Scene A
(High)

Scene B
(Eye-level)
shot

Scene C
(Low
angle)

Scene
D

Scene
E

Column of tanks
on country road

Sc.
A

Sc.
B

Sc.
C

Sc.
D

Sc.
E

What is this?
The enemy?

The sequence is a column of friendly tanks moving up to the front. All the scenes will "cut" well except one. That is Scene E, in which the tanks are moving right to left instead of left to right — like the others! If the movement must change direction, change it during a scene — not a cut.

after the next cut they should see a man walking from right to left, they would assume that two men are walking toward each other. However, if they recognize the man in each scene as being one and the same individual, they will be confused. Did the hero suddenly turn around and walk in the opposite direction, or is the audience being treated to some motion picture hocus-pocus? Neither! The director has merely violated the principle of matching the movement.

The direction of the movement of the subject being photographed must be constant in *relation to the camera*. The background, the terrain in which the scene is being photographed, may or may not have any importance, depending on its recognizable features.

For example: Bill is walking north on a road which has thick woods on both sides. We take a scene of him with the camera on the western side of the road, and on the screen we see him walking *right to left*. In our next scene, Bill is still walking north, but we place the camera on the eastern side of the road. On the screen, Bill walks from *left to right*. If we cut the two scenes together, Bill would seem to change direction, instantly and magically. Our second scene would not "cut" with the first. However, if we had Bill walk south when we moved the camera to the eastern side of the road, on the screen he would still be walking right to left. In spite of the fact that he was actually moving in a different direction, on the screen it would appear to be the same direction, because it was the same direction *in relation to the camera*.

Camera movement presents another problem. As a general rule, it is better not to cut during camera movement. While it is true that the adept editor can handle it occasionally, a cut from a pan or dolly shot to a set shot will frequently cause a definite pictorial jar. It is possible, however, to use a match cut between scenes, both of which have camera movement, if the movement in both scenes is in the same direction and of the same tempo. It is also possible to use a cut-away between a moving shot and a set shot, but it is seldom possible to use a match cut between a moving shot and a set shot.

MATCHING THE LOOK

Matching the look is accomplished by methods similar to those for matching the movement. In movement, the direction of motion of the subject must be the same on each side of the cut. In matching the look, the direction in which a given subject is looking must be the same on each side of the cut.

Let us start with a shot of John talking to Betty. Betty is on the right side of the screen and is looking right to left toward John. John is on the left side and is looking left to right toward Betty. If we cut to a close-up of John, he must be looking, at least slightly, left to right. If we cut to a close-up of Betty, she must be looking right to left. This does not mean, of course, that we need profile composition; * just looking off the proper side of the camera lens is enough.

Remember, if we establish Betty on the right and John on the left, the audience will continue to think of them in that relationship even though we cut to a close-up of one and leave the other out of the picture. Only by moving them in the scene and allowing the audience to observe the changing of position can we reverse them.

Violation of this principle will temporarily confuse the audience and weaken the effectiveness of the story.

THE CUT-AWAY

Despite the best efforts of director, crew, and actors, it sometimes happens that scenes do not match and cannot be cut together without a pictorial jar. When this happens, the editor can usually surmount the difficulty if the director has shot a few cut-aways for the sequence. By properly inserting the cut-away, the editor can momentarily take the audience away from the scene in question. When he gets back to the scene, minor mismatches go unnoticed.

* See definition of composition, pp. 29 and 64.

MATCHING
the LOOK

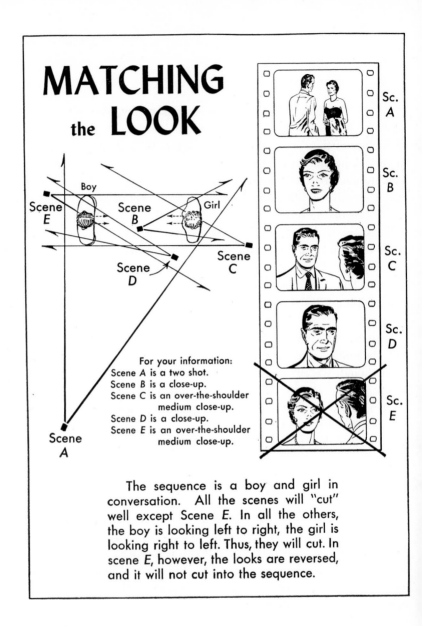

Sc. A

Sc. B

Sc. C

Sc. D

Sc. E

Boy

Scene E

Scene B

Scene D

Scene C

Girl

Scene A

For your information:
Scene A is a two shot.
Scene B is a close-up.
Scene C is an over-the-shoulder
medium close-up.
Scene D is a close-up.
Scene E is an over-the-shoulder
medium close-up.

The sequence is a boy and girl in conversation. All the scenes will "cut" well except Scene E. In all the others, the boy is looking left to right, the girl is looking right to left. Thus, they will cut. In scene E, however, the looks are reversed, and it will not cut into the sequence.

While the cut-away is often useful as a "protection shot," its major use is to guide the audience from subject to subject, and on occasion, to place the audience in the position of one of the actors.

Examine Scenes 2 and 3 of the sample sequence earlier in this chapter. The audience sees John look into the window. Then, in the cut-away, the audience views the rings as John views them. Or look at Scenes 7 and 8. The audience is placed in Mary's position and sees John as she sees him.

A cut-away can also be used to shorten the time necessary to show a given action. By cutting away or into a close-up, we may, for a few seconds, take the audience away from the major action. When the scene again returns to that action, it can be much further advanced without disturbing the continuity. Thus, "film time" becomes much less than actual time.

THE IMAGINARY LINE

The principles of matching are comparatively simple, and most film workers are familiar with them. However, if we have three, four, a dozen, or more people on the set, and if they are moving about, continuously shifting their positions, applying the rules of matching can be somewhat confusing. There is, however, an over-all plan which can be used that will generally assist the director. It is called the *principle of the imaginary line.*

To visualize the imaginary line which crosses the set, think of all the actors and the camera in terms of a plan, a blueprint, or a bird's-eye view. Plot them on paper and draw a line through the two actors, one on each side of the frame, closest to the camera. You cannot properly cut to an angle which would place the camera viewpoint across that line.

It must be understood, however, that there is a difference between the camera and the camera viewpoint. The camera may be moved in a straight line closer to or farther away from the subject without changing the camera viewpoint. Thus, in moving in for a

THE IMAGINARY LINE

Plotting the line:

On a plan view of the master scene, draw a line through the two actors, one on each side of the frame, closest to the camera.

A good principle to know so well you can forget it! – for, like all principles, at times it can be disregarded to good effect!

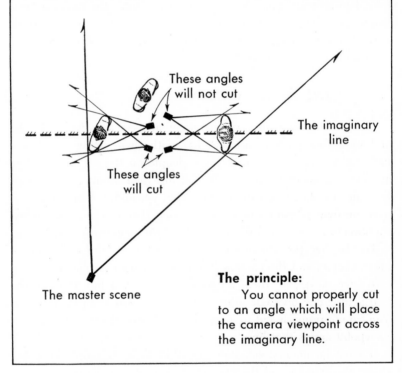

These angles will not cut

These angles will cut

The imaginary line

The master scene

The principle:

You cannot properly cut to an angle which will place the camera viewpoint across the imaginary line.

close-up, the camera itself may be moved across the imaginary line, but the viewpoint of the camera may still be from the same side of the line as the preceding shot. In such a case the principle would not be violated. However, if the second of two shots is such that the camera viewpoint is from the opposite side of the imaginary line from the first shot, the principle has been violated.

Now, if the actors move in the scene, the imaginary line moves with them. If, as they move, they change places with others who become the two actors closest to the camera, the imaginary line also moves and transfers itself to the new subjects. The movement of the actors may even cause the imaginary line to cross over the camera during the scene. That is all right. What was a proper cut at the beginning of the scene would be an improper cut after the line has moved across the camera. The rule of the imaginary line applies only at a given time during the scene; therefore the director must know at what time during a given scene other scenes are expected to cut in.

Just as movement of the subjects may cause the line to pass over the camera, so may camera movement cause the camera to pass over the line. Just after it passes, we have a whole new set of "lefts and rights" to remember in matching movement and look. We cannot cut to another scene which would place the camera viewpoint across the line.

The principle of the imaginary line applies also to the cut-away. We merely draw a line from the subject featured in the previous scene through the subject featured in the cut-away. Both scenes should be photographed from the same side of the line.

Only *during* a scene may the imaginary line be crossed. It cannot be crossed by means of a cut, but only during the scene when subject or camera movement, or a combination of both, causes this theoretical line to move from one side of the camera to the other. Furthermore, the skilled director does not try to avoid this transition. Because movement is interesting and the lifeblood of a good film, the director deliberately plans to keep his subjects moving and his camera moving when necessary, so that seldom will his

THE IMAGINARY LINE
With Movement

For an angle to cut into this part of scene, camera *viewpoint* should not be on this side.

Remember, in applying this principle, that there is a big difference between the camera and the camera *viewpoint*

The camera may be near or far from the subject with the *viewpoint* remaining the same. This may cause the camera, but not the *viewpoint* to cross the line.

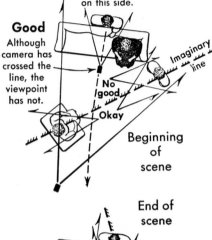

Good
Although camera has crossed the line, the viewpoint has not.

Imaginary line

No good

Okay

Beginning of scene

End of scene

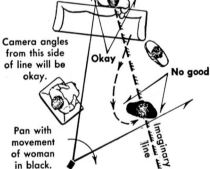

Camera angles from this side of line will be okay.

Okay

No good

Pan with movement of woman in black.

Imaginary line

At any time during a scene there is an imaginary line which should not be crossed to shoot another scene which is expected to cut into the original scene.

scenes be static. Causing the imaginary line to cross over the camera is an additional method of adding interest to the film.

Frequently, in cutting from one scene to another, a perfectly good cut may appear to violate the principle of the imaginary line. If, from a scene containing three or more actors, we cut to one of the actors in the background, we may place the camera in a position which is across the line. However, the *viewpoint* does not cross the line. The camera has merely moved in closer to get a better view, but the same angle could have been photographed if the camera had been moved back to the same side of the line as in the original scene.

It is not meant to imply in this discussion of the imaginary line that on each and every scene the director plots such a line across a plan of his set. Most good directors understand the principle involved so completely that they know instinctively what angles would cross the line.

COMPOSITION AND THE CUT

Most film workers fully realize the necessity of matching the movement, position, and look. However, not too many are aware that the composition of the two scenes involved can influence the smoothness of the cut.

Ordinarily, we think of composition as referring to the balance of the individual picture, the placement of the masses,* the direction of the lines of force.† These things are important, very important, to the effectiveness of the film, and the director who has a good eye for them is fortunate. However, the type of composition we are referring to here has nothing to do with photographic balance and beauty. Rather, it refers to the placing of subjects within the frame so that they will not appear to jump at the time of the cut. In order to accomplish this, four general rules should be observed.

* See definition of balance of masses, p. 66.
† See definition of lines of force, p. 66.

First, *the important subjects should be in the same general area of the frame for each of the two shots which are to be cut together.* If in Scene 5 John is in the upper left of the frame and Mary is in the lower right side, they should remain in the same respective areas in the next scene, Scene 6. Violations of this principle cause the eye to shift quickly at the time of the cut, and the mind is momentarily confused. If Mary is in the lower right of the frame in Scene 6, she should be balanced toward that side of the screen for her close-up in Scene 7.

Observing this principle will sometimes place the director in conflict with his cameraman or director of photography. The cameraman, quite naturally, is interested in photographic beauty and compositional balance. However, it should never be necessary to place a shot off balance in order to avoid violation of this rule. As long as the important subject is not shifted from one side of the screen to the other, no real harm is done. If the problem should become acute, the proper placement of a prop such as a curtain or a piece of furniture will maintain the photographic composition. A cooperative cameraman can usually solve the problem.

The second general rule in composition and the cut is to *change the composition.* It is much better to cut from a long shot to a medium shot, from a close-up to a long shot, or perhaps from a medium shot to a close-up than it is to cut from a long shot to a long shot or from a medium shot to a medium shot.

The third general rule is that *when cutting from an extreme close-up to a longer shot, many mismatches will go unnoticed.* Indeed, from an extreme close-up we may cut to almost anything. While this principle applies to continuity cutting, it is particularly useful in the newsreel-type treatment.

The fourth rule is to *change the angle between scenes.* If the same angle is maintained between a long shot and a medium shot, if the camera shoots along the same axis in both scenes, the most minute mismatches are revealed. It is better to change the angle considerably so that, with the new viewpoint, minor mismatches will go unnoticed. Quite often the smoothest cut results from a *reverse*.

THE REVERSE

Quite probably there is no more misunderstood term in filmdom than the word *reverse*. Many believe that it is a camera angle that reverses the original camera viewpoint, a complete 180-degree turn of the camera axis. If we completely reversed the camera viewpoint, we would get a false reverse, one that would not cut smoothly with the preceding scene.

In the false reverse, the principles of imaginary line and direction of look are violated. The principles of composition and the cut are overlooked, and the entire geography of the set will seem to shift instantly and magically at the time of the cut. Momentarily, at least, the audience will be confused.

In the true reverse, the camera viewpoint will not cross the imaginary line, and the subjects will maintain the same look, camera left or right, depending upon the previous scene from which the reverse must cut.

The most simple example of a reverse is that used when cutting from one to the other of two people facing each other—a boy and a girl, for example—as they engage in a conversation. To establish the action we will probably start with a two shot, the boy on the left, the girl on the right. Then, let us say, we cut to a medium close-up of the girl from over the boy's shoulder. She is a little to the right of screen center and is looking right to left. We see his outline, the side of his face, and his shoulder on the edge and bottom of the screen. Now we cut to a true reverse, a close-up of the boy. He is looking left to right. We call it a reverse, because the camera is pointing in almost the opposite direction from its axis in the previous scene. If we moved the camera around a little further, a 180-degree reverse, so that the boy would look right to left, we would have a false reverse. When viewing this false reverse on the screen, the audience would be momentarily confused.

THE REVERSE

The previous scene
Most principles of editing are concerned with the way a scene "cuts" with the previous scene.

The reverse
It _conforms_ to the principles of matching the look, composition and the cut, and the imaginary line.

The false reverse
It _violates_ the principles of matching the look, composition and the cut, and the imaginary line.

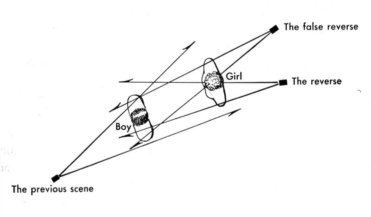

Frequently, a reverse is also a cut-away. Examine again the sample sequence at the beginning of this chapter. Scene 3 is a reverse of Scene 2; Scene 4 is a reverse of Scene 3; Scene 8 is a reverse of Scene 7; Scene 9 is a reverse of Scene 8. In Scene 9 the angle is toward Mary; in Scene 8, it is toward John.

NEWSREEL CUTTING

Thus far we have been considering the cut as applied to the continuity type film or sequence in which the picture must tell the story. In the newsreel-type film, however, the narration tells the story, and the picture is more or less illustrative. Here a completely new set of mechanical cutting rules applies. Because it is usually impossible to match any action, it is necessary that scenes to be cut together be as unlike as possible. Almost every scene is a cut-away. The cut must tell the audience instantly, "This is a completely new scene and bears no continuity of action with the previous scene." The narrator or sound effects must carry the continuity of thought, tying together the two scenes.

In the newsreel-type film, cutting together extreme long shots, extreme close-ups, cut-aways, and odd angle shots is the rule rather than the exception. When we can, we match action and approach a form of pictorial continuity, but when that is impossible, we make no such attempt. Instead we cut our scenes together with such vast changes between scenes that the audience is instantly aware of the new approach. Thought continuity is carried by the audio.

As pointed out previously, the newsreel technique is frequently used in all types of films. Indeed, together with the montage,* which will be discussed in Chapter Four, it is an ideal method of condensing much action or a long period of time into a few minutes of film. In the Academy Award winner, *The Snake Pit*, this technique was used to great advantage. The director must understand it, as well as continuity cutting.

Yes, the director must understand both newsreel and continuity

* See definition of montage, p. 56.

cuts so well that he can use them as a tool without giving thought to the mechanical rules. The operation of the tool is fundamental; using the tool to build the film is art. The director who knows his rules of cutting so well that he understands when he can violate them to advantage, so well that he concentrates not on cutting but on his story, his theme, his crew, and his actors—that is the director who has solved his first and foremost problem. He knows the rules, but he also knows it is people, not rules, who create motion picture films.

CHAPTER THREE

MOVEMENT

The life of the film director would be simple indeed if we could put down a set of rules by which he could plan and direct his films. Instead, he must deal primarily with imaginative ideas and people who sometimes tend to be a little less than practical. He is given a story, a piece of imagination expressed in words, and from it he must direct the production of many individual scenes on film, which, when cut together in the proper order, will give that story interest, realism, life, breadth, and meaning.

Interest has many phases. At one extreme we have the passing interest which merely keeps the audience from getting up and walking out of the theater. At the other extreme we have the interest which results from a theme so well presented that the audience is emotionally upset for days and even goaded into "doing something" about the social, educational, or economic problem presented. Let us start from the beginning and discover some of the things which cause a mere passing interest, a passing interest which must be sustained if it is to build into something greater.

Naturally, there must be a story or theme—probably both. The actors must be convincing, and the staging and photographic techniques of the director must in themselves be interesting and in keeping with the mood.

The staging techniques of all directors seem to have one thing in common. That is an intelligent use of movement.

REASONS FOR MOVEMENT

In the well-staged film, actors do not just sit and talk, nor does the narrator drone on while the audience gazes at some static piece of scenery. If actors are talking in a drawing room, one of them gets up from his chair and takes a cigarette from the table. As he lights it, he walks across the room and leans against the fireplace. The other actor follows with his eyes, and later does some bit of business which keeps the scene moving and interesting. The scene is kept alive; as the actors move they give the camera new perspectives, new angles, which together with other scenes that are cut into the sequence never allow the audience to become bored with one viewpoint.

The possibilities for movement and change are limitless—the variations the good director can utilize are literally uncountable. However, we can examine some of the general patterns together with their uses, and from them possibly discover the type of thinking which the director must employ.

We already know that the director has available two general types of movement: camera movement and subject movement. Of these two, the first depends upon the latter. As a general rule, camera movement is held to a minimum and used only when subject movement makes it necessary. We pan, tilt, or truck only for a reason, and usually that reason is the movement of the subjects. Therefore, we plan subject movement so that camera movement will be interesting, varied, and follow the rhythm and tempo of the story. We think of one as we think of the other, and we plan one as we plan the other. Both types of movements, camera and subject, depend upon and complement each other. The pattern of one is the pattern of the other.

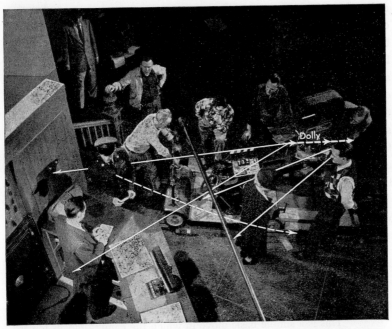

(U.S. Army Photo)

Shooting a dolly shot. The grip is getting ready to push the dolly which rides on the metal tracks. At this point, the scene is a two shot of the desk clerk and the sergeant. Later, the sergeant will leave the desk, and the camera will truck with him and come to rest on a closeup of the lady. The movement is a variation of basic move 6.

Before we examine some of the basic patterns, let us enumerate some of the purposes behind movement: to move from a long or medium shot to a closer view of the subject; to move from a close view of a subject to a longer shot; to transfer attention from one subject or group of subjects, to another subject or group of subjects; to vary the composition and move the subjects for pace and tempo; to maintain a close view of a subject or subjects while they are in motion; and to lead into and sometimes take the place of opticals at the beginning or end of a sequence.

Generally, subjects should move toward or away from the camera, either directly or at an angle. If a subject moves directly toward the camera, from a long shot to a close-up, it is usually possible to film the scene without any appreciable camera movement. Much more frequently, however, the subject will move at an angle toward or away from the camera. In this event, it is usually necessary to pan or truck with the subject in order that the composition may at all times be balanced. The most pleasing move is usually that of the subject moving at an angle toward or away from the camera, and the camera pans or trucks, sometimes both, unnoticeably, but enough to maintain composition and change the background of the scene.

These, then, are the reasons for movement and the changes for which we strive. Let us now look at the major patterns from which are evolved the unlimited variations we see on the theatrical screen.

TWELVE BASIC MOVEMENTS

1. *The truck-in (or dolly-in)*

    This is a simple basic move in which the camera moves toward a stationary subject or object. Its use is usually limited to narrowing the attention of the audience to a particular person or item and at the same time maintaining the subject's geographical position on the set.

2. *The truck-out (or dolly-out)*

    Just the opposite of the truck-in. Sometimes it is used to open a sequence when a particular item has significant meaning to the sequence to follow. At other times it may follow a truck-in which closed the preceding sequence.

3. *The walk-in*

    A transition from a medium shot or long shot to a closer shot by having the subject move toward the camera.

4. *The walk-away*

    The opposite of the walk-in. A transition from a close-up to a medium or long shot by having the subject move away from the camera.

An Example of
A BASIC MOVE

6. Following one subject to reveal and concentrate on another subject; original subject exits.

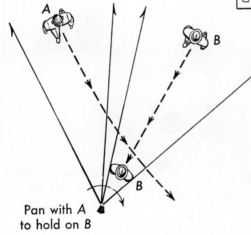

An effective method of transferring attention from *A* to *B*

A

B

B

Pan with *A* to hold on *B*

An Example of
A BASIC MOVE

7. **Following** one
   subject to include
   more subjects

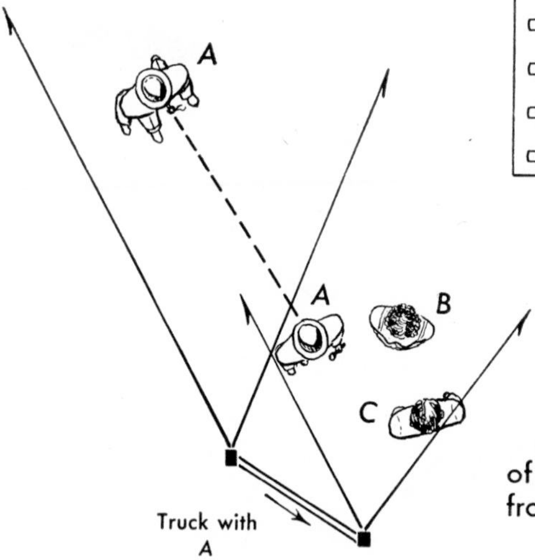

A common method
of expanding interest
from one to a group

Truck with
A

5. *The follow shot*

Both subject and camera move. Here, the camera trucks along with a moving subject and maintains approximately the same composition on the subject, but the background changes. Very short follow shots may be executed with a pan instead of a truck, but the composition of the moving subject will change.

6. *Following one subject to reveal and concentrate on another subject; original subject exits*

In the beginning of the movement, a pan or a truck follows a subject. A new subject appears from the foreground or background. The camera centers on the new subject as the original subject exits. This is an effective method of transferring interest smoothly from one subject to another.

7. *Following one subject to include more subjects*

This kind of movement is similar to the preceding type except that the original subject does not exit from the scene. It is a common method of expanding interest from one to a group.

8. *Transition from a group to an individual*

This movement can be executed by any one of several different means. One method is simply a variation of the walk-in, in which one subject in a group walks toward the camera and into a sharp-focus close-up. The original group of subjects now merges into out-of-focus background, and attention is centered on the individual in the close-up.

Another method begins as a follow shot of a group and then narrows to a follow shot of an individual in the group. Usually, this is accomplished by the simple expedient of having the subjects move faster than the camera, thus causing the camera to move closer to the group and narrow the field to one subject.

9. *Following a subject leaving a group*

The beginning of this type of movement is a shot including several subjects. One of them walks away from the others; the camera pans or trucks with him, and the other subjects are excluded from the scene.

An Example of
A BASIC MOVE

11. Subjects
    reversing

As girl
moves,
boy
turns.

Girl moves
forward
and turns
to face
boy.

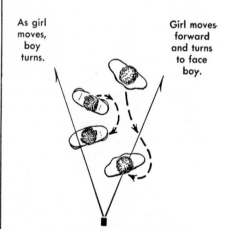

Camera may have
to pan and/or truck
to maintain composition

This accomplishes in
movement what the reverse
does in cutting.

However, the reverse
takes two setups; this
takes one.

10. *Correcting for composition*

> The camera must either pan, tilt, or truck slightly in order to maintain composition on one or more moving subjects. For example, we have a medium close-up of a man seated in a chair. He rises, and in order to hold him in the picture and keep a balanced frame, the camera either tilts up with him as he rises or trucks back to include more area.

11. *Subjects reversing*

> This accomplishes in movement what the reverse does in cutting. The camera is shooting past *A* and featuring *B*. *B* walks toward the camera, past *A*, and turns to face *A*, *B*'s back to the camera. *A* turns toward the camera to follow the movement of *B*. Now, *A* is being featured. To maintain composition, the camera may pan or truck with the movement.

12. *Countering*

> One subject moves and another subject "counters" or moves into a predetermined position which will maintain picture composition.

A study of the foregoing basic moves will reveal that they are very closely allied and in some cases actually interrelated. *Correcting for composition* is actually *countering* by the camera. *Transition from a group to an individual* is much the same as *following a subject leaving a group*, the only difference being that in one the group remains in the scene, in the other it does not.

We must not think of these moves as distinct and separate items which the director can pull out of his bag of tricks when he needs them. Rather, one is part of another; one can lead to another. A variation of one may become a form of another, which, in turn, may lead into a completely new variation.

One thing, however, is common to practically all moves. With the possible exceptions of the *truck-in* and the *truck-out*, each requires synchronous camera and subject movement. Unless an unusual camera effect is desired, camera movement should be so synchronized with subject movement that the audience is never aware of the pan, the tilt, or the truck. When the subject moves, the camera moves; when the subject stops, the camera stops; and the audience, concentrating on the subject, is unaware of the camera movement. Harmony between them results in a fluidity and grace which follows the tempo of the action. This is the perfection for which the director strives. Unfortunately, mechanical or human failures often cause the movement to fall short of perfection.

DIFFICULTIES OF MOVEMENT

In order to execute almost any of the moves, there must be perfect timing among actors and crew. The move becomes even more difficult when it requires a truck or a dolly. The *grips*, the men who push the dolly, must time their moves with the moves of the actors. The actors must time their moves with those of each other and must move at the same tempo in rehearsals and take. The operating cameraman must time his pans and tilts with both actors and grips. The move probably requires a change of focus, so the assistant cameraman, the man who turns the lens ring on the camera, must synchronize his moves with those of all the others. Thus, many scenes requiring both subject and camera movement necessitate numerous rehearsals, and seldom are they secured on the first take.

All this, of course, requires time and film which cost money. It is small wonder, then, that some of the financially limited producing organizations absolutely prohibit dolly shots. Fortunately, however, there are methods and means by which the director can make the dolly shot economical as well as artistic. In later chapters, we shall discuss some of them.

THE MASTER SCENE

Let us return, for a moment, to a consideration of the cut. In shooting a sequence, a director does not shoot only the angles necessary and plan for the exact spot in the action where the cuts will take place. Rather, he gives considerable overlap of

Preparing to shoot a boom shot of Jean Simmons for *Androcles and the Lion,* directed by Chester Erskine. Moving shots like this are among the most difficult that camera crews are called upon to make.

action in the adjoining scenes so that the editor may have a choice as to the exact spot for making the cut.

Frequently, the director will shoot the entire sequence from a longer angle and then repeat short segments of the action for medium shots and close-ups. The scene which includes all the action of the sequence, or section of the sequence, is called a *master scene.* The closer angles of segments of the action are called *cut-ins.* They cut in to the master scene.

Now, if the director, in planning his master scene, makes good use of the principles of movement, he can frequently eliminate individual set-ups and cuts to secure his cut-ins. Instead, the transitions in the movement cause the change from longer shot to close-up and back again.

The planning and staging of his master scenes is one of the director's most important jobs. It is in the staging of the master scene and the selection and placing of the cut-ins that the director secures editorial tempo and timing in movement and cutting.

MOVEMENT AND TASTE

Aside from economic reasons, camera movement must be used with discretion and taste. A good film does have movement, but that movement is paced with the tempo of the story, and restful pauses of stationary dialogue or facial reaction will interest the audience far more than a see-sawing camera and actors who seem to be imbued with perpetual motion. Indeed, some directors have become so interested in movement for movement's sake that their films have lost their dramatic effect, and audiences have become so involved in watching "technique" that the story has been almost lost.

An experiment in movement was conducted by Alfred Hitchcock in his direction of *Rope*. This film was practically devoid of cuts except where necessary to join the thousand-foot rolls of film. All transitions were secured through camera and subject movement. While interesting as an experiment, it certainly blazed no trails in camera and staging technique. It did, however, open up new production procedures and methods of rehearsing actors, and for this reason, if for no other, it probably was worth the effort.

Good film-staging technique is a tasteful blending of camera and subject movement, reverses, close-ups, long shots, and almost static scenes in which dialogue, sound effect, or an actor's expression carries the interest. Above all, the use of each technique must have as a purpose the amplification of the over-all effectiveness of the film, and the change from one to another should have a rhythm and pace of its own—just as much as a piece of music or a stanza of well-written poetry.

CHAPTER FOUR

ART AND VISUAL TECHNIQUE

Our definition of art changes as our powers of perception change. However, for basic discussion purposes, we may tentatively define it as creative work which influences the emotions.

Techniques might be defined as methods of construction used in building a creative work. Thus, art is achieved when the techniques of a creative work are so blended that people are moved to tears, laughter, or excitement.

Whether the creative work be an oil painting, a musical score, a piece of literature, or a motion picture film makes little difference. The true test of any original work is the influence it has on the emotions. The methods used within the art form to influence these emotions are merely techniques of the creator.

In films, many techniques are combined to influence the audience. The story; the theme and its universality, or its pointed approach to a particular type of spectator; the sincerity of the acting; the staging and visual techniques of the director; the honesty of the sets and props; the photographic lighting; and the composition of the individual scenes—all these factors can influence the emotions of the audience. In a good film or a great film, they are so interdependent that they can hardly be separated. Each depends upon and supplements the other, and it is the sum total of their effects that grips the audience. Magnificent dialogue and acting performed upon a bare Shakespearean stage will excite the intellectual curiosity of select audiences. But that is not the purpose of the motion picture film. The motion picture should be a journey into reality, the audience should live the experience, it should become a part of the story. But the medium can achieve that reality only when the varied techniques of the many crafts engaged in making the film are perfectly blended. Thus, the visual techniques employed by the director depend upon the mood, the theme, and the actors. The same techniques when employed with one sequence will secure one result; in another sequence they will have an entirely different result.

There are four basic visual techniques which can be used to influence the emotions. Two of them, the cut and movement, are basic continuity techniques. The other two, composition and lighting, are primarily audience-appeal techniques. The first two are planned by the director and executed or controlled, in great measure, by the editor. The latter two are planned by the director and executed, to a great extent, by the cameraman. Thus, to achieve the fullest measure of perfection, the director must be a leader as well as an artist, and the editor and the cameraman must be cooperative workers as well as artistic technicians. While the director can conceive the visual plan, he must depend upon others for its execution. He must always remember, "No *one* person can make a film."

THE CUT

It is the editor, or cutter, whose job it is to influence the emotions through cutting. If the editor is not well versed in his art or aware of his responsibility, the greatest direction can be wasted. On the other hand, the editor is limited by the film which the director gives him, and he must look to the director for a certain amount of guidance. The director, therefore, must "feel" instinctively what type of cutting is best suited to any particular mood, and he must so stage and photograph his film.

Naturally enough, cutting techniques are closely tied in with movement and composition. Movement and composition may be superbly executed during production, but to influence the emotions of the audience each scene must be fitted into its proper place in the sequence. The serenity and smoothness of placid camera and subject movement can lull the audience into a calm, peaceful mood, but if a few odd-angle scenes are cut into the sequence, the mood will become more tense, more exciting.

The placing and number of cuts have a very direct bearing on the "pace" of a sequence. The more cuts, the faster it is paced and the more exciting it becomes. The tempo of the movement also influences the emotions. The problem is to use the number of cuts that suits the tempo of the movement. No rule can be given for this; it is entirely a matter of the picture sense and inherent feeling for rhythm of the director and editor. Increasing the number of cuts and shortening the length of scenes build up physical excitement. Violent changes of angles, disregard of the composition and cut principle—*impact*—can intensify this excitement.

Extreme physical excitement, such as that in a battle sequence, is built up by gradually shortening the length of scenes as the action mounts. Near the climax, one scene comes almost on top of another. Long shots—close-ups—odd angle shots—extreme low angles—high angles—they follow each other with the increasing rapidity and tempo of the mounting action. Then, as the climax is reached, the scenes become longer, the audience has more time to study them, and the tension eases.

Fewer cuts, longer scenes, and less impact in the few cuts remaining induce a calmer reaction. However, if the scenes become too long and the cuts too few, if the absence of camera movement holds the same perspective while the action builds emotionally, the audience will unconsciously transfer their impatience for a new scene, a new viewpoint, to impatience for an outlet for their rising emotion. In this way we can help build impatience by holding overly long on the same scenes.

It must be understood that we have been stating generalizations, and they cannot even be interpreted as rules. Only ability, appreciation, and experience can decide just which technique to use at a given time and how best to portray a given story. It is for this reason that no book can teach a man how to direct films; it can only help him to understand a director's problems.

MOVEMENT

The intelligent use of movement is one of the director's foremost visual techniques. With it, he can make the audience feel ill at ease, help build the personalities of the characters, give the audience a sense of well-being, induce an air of mystery, or help create a gay, scintillating mood.

For example, a repeated use of the walk-in when moving from a medium shot to a close-up can help impress the audience with the extrovert nature of one of the actors. The actor moves toward the audience just as his inner nature radiates toward his associates.

If we seek the opposite effect, that is, to emphasize the introvert nature of an actor, we use camera movement when we move from a longer shot to a close-up. We force the audience to move toward him to become acquainted.

Slow, graceful subject and camera movement, in perfect coordination, gives the audience a sense of well-being, while camera and subject movement not perfectly synchronized strikes a discordant note, and the audience may feel slightly ill at ease. This latter technique must be used with extreme discretion, however, or what is meant to influence the emotions will simply appear like poor execution. In using imperfect movement, it is seldom necessary to resort to bad composition, nor is it wise to destroy the basic pace of the action. Indeed, both camera and subject movement are planned or conceived in the normal manner, but in the execution, the camera is allowed to anticipate or lag behind subject movement. The result, if this technique is properly carried out, is a vague uneasiness on the part of the audience.

Rarely does the director use camera movement without subject movement. Sometimes, however, this technique may be used to accomplish a particular purpose. In the proper setting, moving the camera slowly over inanimate objects can help induce an air of mystery. Accustomed to life and subject movement, the eye unconsciously searches for some pertinent action. Sometimes, too, the camera can simulate the roving eyes of one of the actors and thus place the audience in the position of that actor. Called "the subjective camera," this technique was used for an entire film in Robert Montgomery's *Lady in the Lake* and received fairly favorable reception. Generally, however, the subjective camera is used only in isolated scenes such as a cut-away from the principal action.

Like the cut, camera movement should be paced to suit the action and the mood. Fast movement is bright, gay, and exciting, while slow movement can be sad, full of suspense, or placid and calm, depending on the story.

All movements in themselves are meaningless. Within a given story, certain movements will heighten the mood while certain others may lessen it or give it a different shade of emotional meaning. In one circumstance, a given movement may have one effect, while in another circumstance it may have an entirely different effect. The problem of the director is to know which movements will help induce the emotion desired, and this problem, like questions as to the proper use of the cut, can be solved only with ability, appreciation, and experience.

COMPOSITION

Within the limits of the personality and working pattern of the director, the cameraman or director of photography sets up, or improves, the composition of each shot. Since the director sets up the editorial pattern, he must choose or approve each angle, but the cameraman, as the photographic specialist, helps improve the framing and perspective. Therefore, the cameraman should have studied the scenario and be well acquainted with the emotional reaction the director wishes to secure from each sequence. Composition has a marked emotional appeal, and the good cameraman can have a great influence on the dramatic worth of the film. Furthermore, as the director plans his shooting angles and editorial pattern, he must consider the influence that composition can have on the audience.

One of the finest examples of compositional influence can be seen in the British film, *The Fallen Idol.* As a small boy's story, the greater part of it is photographed from the eye level of a small boy. The audience sees the world, inhabited by enormous giants and full of oversized buildings and rooms, much the same as the little hero sees it.

It is not the purpose of this chapter to study good and bad composition. Rather we are interested here in the types of good composition which will produce given emotional results.

The study of composition has two general aspects, the angle and the framing. The angle refers to the direction in which the camera is pointed; the framing refers to the amount of material included in the shot and its placement within the frame.

The angle of a shot has a marked influence on the audience's psychological reaction to the subject matter photographed. As demonstrated in *The Fallen Idol*, angles shooting upward cause the subject matter to appear stronger, more powerful, than the audience. Angles shooting downward give the audience a feeling of strength and make the subject appear weaker.

The hackneyed situation so common to old-time melodramas may serve as an example. An automobile is stranded on the railroad track. Shooting upward at the approaching locomotive and slightly down on the stalled automobile emphasizes the relationship of the two. The thundering train is about to destroy the frail auto. Suppose, however, the same train were approaching a washed-out bridge. A downward angle on the train gives the audience a feeling of superiority and sympathy for that which is about to be

Shooting upward gives strength to the subject, as demonstrated by this low angle shot from *The Story of Robin Hood.* The film was directed by Ken Annakin and distributed by RKO.

destroyed. Here, too, framing can be used to advantage by showing the train from a distance in order to play down the tremendous power which would be evident in a close-up.

Another example might be a situation wherein the heavy is about to murder one of the supporting players. Shooting from slightly below eye level on the criminal and slightly above eye level on the victim emphasizes the relationship of the two.

As a general rule, the angle, or viewpoint level, should be approximately that of an individual standing or sitting, as the case may be. Variations above or below this level need not be extreme. Shooting down past the chandelier or up across the shoe tops are shots reserved primarily for shock effect—and they should be reserved for that. The more extreme the angle, the more violent the shock.

Orson Welles, in his first film, *Citizen Kane*, used violent angles and extreme composition to such a point that they lost their effectiveness. The audience had become so accustomed to extremes that they failed to produce the desired result when they were really necessary. By the third reel, many were more interested in the bizarre composition of the individual shots than in the theme of the film. Odd angles, which are jarring emotionally and can be used to build suspense, are necessary, but their use should be limited to their need. Thus, during the building of emotions, it is often better to take a normal or near-normal viewpoint and frame or partially obstruct the view with a foreground prop or bit of foreground action. While this may have but little shock effect, it does give the audience a sense of annoyance which paves the way for the crescendo of emotion to come later. It is then that violent angles should be used.

The framing of the shot also influences the emotions. Closer shots usually make the action more personal, while longer shots place the audience in the position of a spectator. Extreme close-ups of faces tend to tug at the emotions and build up excitement. Cutting from long shot to close-up adds impact.

Certain types of long shots can have a peculiarly sympathetic appeal. A sympathetic character, a single small figure in the screen, dwarfed by overpowering conditions of nature or man-made surroundings, has about him a helplessness that induces audience-sympathy. Many of the early Chaplin pictures used this device to good effect. In *The Breaking Point*, Michael Curtiz used it in the last scene of the film to excellent advantage. Fred Zinnemann also made use of it in *High Noon* to emphasize the loneliness of deserted law man, Gary Cooper.

If his is to be an effective film which will hold and influence people, the director must weigh all factors each time the cameras roll. The angle and framing of each scene must be composed not only for good mechanical cutting continuity, but, in addition, in such a way that the cutting, the movement, and the composition will contribute to the over-all emotional effect desired.

LIGHTING

The lighting of each scene is entirely under the technical direction of the cameraman. It is he—part artist, part technician, part gang boss—who tells the electricians where to put their lights so that the blending of light and dark, shadow and highlight, will present the action in the technical perfection of modern photography. Just as the brush strokes of the master painter can create an emotional mood so, too, can the lights and shadows of the photographer. Whether the image is in color or black and white, the mood of the lighting must correspond to the mood of the story.

This is a powerful technique that the cameraman has at his disposal, and it must be blended with all the other techniques which contribute to the art of the film. The cameraman should read and study the scenario, learn to know the actors, and draw out of the director as much as he can of the directorial treatment and plan for interpreting the story idea. On the other hand, it is the director's responsibility to understand that for which the cameraman is striving and to give him all the help possible. He must know what type of lighting is best suited to the mood he desires, and he must plan the action to help facilitate that type of lighting.

In general, a low key, or predominance of dark areas, is most effective for the mysterious or dramatic. A high key, or predominance of light areas, is usually most effective for comedy, or gay, frivolous moods. The entire range between these two extremes is available for the matching of any given mood.

The methods by which the cameraman secures any given lighting key are not particularly important to the director. However, the placing of the camera, the layout of the set or location, interior light sources such as windows and lights, the location of the sun, and the tonal values of interior walls have a direct bearing on the cameraman's problems. Now, in order to attain a smooth visual continuity and complete subject-camera coordination, the director must be responsible for the camera angle and approximate framing. He must, however, if he expects to secure the most from his cameraman, consult him and comply with his wishes as much as possible. In solving their joint problems, they must both remember that photographic lighting is important to the film they are making, but it is only one of the techniques which help make up the picture.

Since certain cameramen are more skilled in the use of low-key lighting and certain others in the use of high-key, it is obvious that the choice of a cameraman for the film is of considerable importance. All too often, however, the director has little to say about crew assignments. It frequently happens that prior commitments or, in the larger studios, scheduling conditions make proper assignments almost impossible. It is here that the producer or studio executive can be of the utmost assistance. With the proper crew for the proper picture, the director's job is half done.

THE MONTAGE

When it is desirable to cover a considerable period of time or sequence of action in a short length of film and at the same time to leave the audience with a particular emotional experience, the *montage* may be used. The montage is a succession of miscellaneous short scenes, unlike pictorially, but which together, with sound effects and music, convey a desired thought or emotional pattern.

Occasionally a montage is put together by means of short, fast cuts, but usually it is formed by a blend of dissolves, wipes, and superimposures. Sometimes as many as three or four scenes are visible at one time. One scene dissolves into another and still another, while other scenes, superimposed, wipe off and on in a variety of patterns. In up and down wipes of miscellaneous designs, moving diagonally and straight across, expanding and contracting, swinging and spinning, the scenes wipe off and on and dissolve in and out like the wandering visions of a tortured mind.

Some of the finest montages I have seen were in *The Snake Pit*, Anatole Litvak's great film of the experiences of a mental patient. Too, in *Journey to Reality*, an army documentary directed by Charley Turner, the exceptional montage work dealt with abnormal psychology. In the case of the latter film, Turner and his editor, Eric Lawrence, worked together so closely that, when the film was finished, neither knew just what ideas each had contributed.

Sometimes the montage is decided upon after the film has been photographed, and the editor then must make use of stock material, duplicates of film already used, and out-takes which would otherwise land on the cutting room floor. Usually, however, it is well planned in advance, and, in some of the larger studios, certain editors do only montage work.

Since, in the montage, it is not necessary to plan angles and frame the composition with continuity cutting in mind, full advantage can be taken of the influence of movement and composition on the emotions. Bizarre angles and extreme close-ups lose part of their shock effect if introduced by an optical rather than a cut; therefore these types of composition can often be used in the extreme in the optical montage. When it is desired to increase the shock effect, the length of the individual optical can be shortened to produce almost the effect of a cut.

BLENDING OF TECHNIQUES

We must remember that the use of the visual techniques, by themselves, means nothing. To produce the desired results, they must be blended with the mood, the action, the acting, the sound effects, and the music. Otherwise they are merely "techniques" in the most material sense. Their true worth is only apparent in their tasteful coordination and in the ultimate living experience of the audience.

We must remember, too, that it is almost impossible to explain with mere words the visual experience which will produce an emotional result. Who can describe the smile of the "Mona Lisa" or the power of Niagara? Most directors feel a mood so strongly that its visual interpretation is almost inherent in their very being. Yet, if we should ask them why one technique will be inappropriate in a given sequence, their explanation might seem quite illogical. They feel the answer, they know it to be true, but they can express it only in their own visual medium.

Yes, in any art, the artist's *feeling* is often more important than his thinking. This might seem like an excuse for mystification, but if we need proof of its truth we need only remember the fevered minds of some of the greatest artists whose work has come down to us through history. While it may take the logic of science to make possible the modern film, its true worth is often the result of the hypersensitive emotions of its authors.

CHAPTER FIVE

ABOUT CAMERA

Do you remember, as a child, the little stamp-sized book-lets which you used to flip with your thumb in order to see a bit of moving action? Each page had an individual drawing almost like the preceding one, yet slightly different. Those successive differences from page to page were the different stages of the movement you saw when the pages were caused to turn rapidly. The optical illusion which gave apparent movement to still drawings is the same illusion which gives apparent movement to a series of projected still pictures, and it is the simple principle upon which the multi-million-dollar film industry is based. Each page in the booklet functioned in the same way as each picture in a strip of motion picture film. In professional 35mm. film there are sixteen such pictures to the foot, and the film runs through the camera and projector at twenty-four pictures—or frames—per second, or ninety feet per minute.

The technical aspects of the motion picture camera or of the cameraman's job are of little interest to the director, but many phases of photographic work do relate to directorial problems. Lenses, composition, camera operation, lighting, rear screen photography—all of these things come within the scope of the camera-man's work, but they must be understood by the director. The better he understands them, the more the job of each will be simplified.

LENSES

The lens transmits the light reflected to it by the subject and forms an image of it on the film. The physics and chemistry of that operation have little relationship to film directing, and complicated theories of optics and light are no concern of the director. However, the director should understand the practical limitations and capabilities of the camera lens as a tool with which any desired composition can be secured. With the lens, the cameraman may make objects appear closer together or farther apart than they really are; he may alter the perspective of a given scene; he may center attention by means of focus; he may control exposure to gain lighting effect.

Lenses vary from short focal lengths to long focal lengths or so-called telescopic lenses. The *focal length* of a lens refers to the distance from the surface of the film to the optical center of the lens. The shorter the focal length, the larger the area the lens will photograph from a given camera position; and vice versa, the longer the focal length, the smaller the area the lens will include in the shot. The obvious result is that short focal-length lenses make objects appear farther away while long focal-length lenses seem to bring objects closer.

The focal length of a lens can also control the apparent relative sizes of different objects within a shot and the apparent distance between them. This relationship is known as *perspective*. A short focal-length lens may increase the apparent distance between near objects and far objects. It will also increase the apparent size of an interior room set. A long focal-length lens may make the distance between near objects and far objects appear less than it actually is.

The professional 35mm. motion picture camera has a wide selec-

THE SHORT focal-length lens

It separates foreground and background and increases the apparent size of a set.

It has a longer depth of field

THE LONG focal-length lens

It brings foreground and background closer together.

It has a shorter depth of field

tion of lenses. Most used are the 25mm., the 35mm., the 40mm., the 50mm. or two-inch, and the 75mm. or three-inch lens. The two-inch lens most nearly approximates the perspective of the human eye, although the "angle of visual perception" of that lens is considerably less. Those lenses of a focal length shorter than two inches are generally referred to as *wide angle lenses.*

Lenses are also classified according to the maximum amount of light they will transmit. This, of course, depends upon the diameter of the lens in relation to its focal length. In the lens barrel there is an iris diaphragm which can be opened or closed to control the amount of light transmitted; this opening or closing is calibrated in f or T numbers called stops. For simplicity, in our discussion, we shall refer to them as f numbers.

Now, the lower the f number, the greater the lens opening, the more light it will transmit, and the less light will be needed on the subject for a proper exposure. Lenses are designated by their lowest f number. Thus, a lens may be an f:2, an f:3.5, or an f:5.6 lens. They are also designated, as we know, by their focal length. Thus, a complete designation might be a 40mm. f:2.5 lens or a 35mm. f:2.3 lens.

The image produced by the lens is critically sharp in only one plane which can be changed as desired by turning the lens in its spiral mount. On either side of this plane of critical focus is a region within which images are so slightly out of focus that they are acceptable. This region is called *depth of field.*

Under certain conditions, the depth of field can be increased. The greater the distance of the point of focus from the camera, the greater is the depth of field. The smaller the distance from the camera to the point of focus, the smaller is the depth of field. Furthermore, the focal length of the lens influences the depth of field. The smaller the focal length of the lens, the greater is the depth of field, and the longer the focal length of the lens, the smaller is the depth of field. Telescopic lenses have very short depths of field.

The lens opening also affects the depth of field. The smaller the opening or higher the f number, the greater will be the depth of field, and, of course, the lower the *f* number, the smaller it will be.

Thus, a short focal-length lens, say a 25mm., shooting in brilliant light at *f*:11 and focused at twenty feet will have a depth of field extending from three feet in front of the camera to infinity. On the other hand, a three-inch lens, shooting in interior light at *f*:4, and focused at four feet will be acceptably sharp only from approximately three feet and ten inches to four feet and two inches —only four inches. Everything else will be progressively blurred and out of focus.

It might seem that a limited depth of field is a disadvantage. Usually it is, but often it can be quite the opposite. Many times the director uses it to center the attention upon a particular point in the screen or even to lead the eye from one object to another. For example, suppose we have a medium close-up of the leading lady. In the background, out of focus, is a door. The door opens, and the leading man enters. For dramatic reasons, we desire that the audience see the man before the lady is aware of his presence. Thus, the focus is shifted from her in the foreground to the man in the background. A second or so later, the lady becomes aware of him and turns to face him. We now have the conventional over-the-shoulder shot featuring the man. The lady, with her back to the camera, is intentionally in soft focus, and the eyes of the audience are led to the man who is in sharp focus and facing the camera.

However, suppose we have a scene with both of them in it from the beginning. Engaged in a vitriolic conversation, the lady has her back turned to the man. The camera is on an off-center close-up of the lady, and in the background we see the figure of the man. In this situation, in order to hold both characters sharp, it is necessary to secure extreme depth of focus. A very wide angle lens plus plenty of light will enable us to use a small lens opening and will probably do the trick.

The wide angle lens has come into considerable use in recent years because of its peculiar ability to increase the scope of a set, to simplify the focus problem, and to film striking angles with extreme foreground action while the center of interest is in the back-ground. The first outstanding job of this nature was done by cameraman Gregg Toland in Orson Welles's *Citizen Kane.*

Although the selection and operation of the lens is the job of the cameraman, this limited discussion is included because the director must understand its basic capabilities and limitations. The director who understands the lens will not only ease the job of the cameraman but will help him secure that type of composition and photography best suited to the story, the mood, and the editorial pattern. A director and a cameraman who understand each other's problems, who do not infringe on each other's jobs but instead work in complete harmony and understanding, compose a production team that is hard to beat.

COMPOSITION

Composition is the placement of objects within the photographic frame. There are many types of composition, and tastes and ideas vary widely. There are rules to be followed—and on occasion to be broken.

Frequently, the best composition is secured by photographers who know little of the theories and rules governing it. Rather they have almost an inborn sense of what is pleasing; they have what might be called "an eye for composition." A short discussion of some of the principles underlying composition may help develop appreciation in those who unfortunately have no such "eye."

The frame of the motion picture screen has been admirably designed for good composition. Not nearly as pleasing as its rectangular shape is the square or circular outline. For a time, television set manufacturers made an attempt to popularize the circular screen, but because of its poor adaptability to pleasing composition it failed to appeal to the public. The wide screen, at present being developed by the major theatrical studios, also suffers from lack of compositional appeal. The rectangular screen itself is an example of one of the foremost rules of composition, the Rule of Thirds.

(Courtesy of RKO Radio Pictures, Inc.)

Two shots that illustrate the Rule of Thirds. Both from the same sequence in *The Big Sky*, directed by Howard Hawks, they also demonstrate the principle of matching the movement. In both, the movement is right to left.

The Rule of Thirds refers to the placement of prominent objects, masses, or lines within the frame. In its most elementary form the rule simply means that it is best not to place the center of interest in the geometrical center of the frame—that symmetrical balance is not desirable. To illustrate, draw the outline of a screen, say a rectangle four by five inches. Now, draw two vertical lines through that rectangle so as to divide it into three smaller rectangles. Next, draw two horizontal lines across so as to divide it into three horizontal parts, or nine still smaller rectangles. The dominant lines of any picture should run approximately along some of these lines, and the lines should be near the dividing margin between masses of dark and light areas.

The Rule of Thirds also applies to the balance of masses. Masses, in this case, refer to particularly light or dark areas. In a low-key scene, the frame should have approximately two-thirds of its area in a dark tone; one-third should be in a contrasting light tone. In a higher-key scene, one-third should be in a low tone while two-thirds should be in a lighter tone. If the balance is half and half, the scene seems to lose interest.

Every picture should have one center of interest, that is, a point to which the eye of the viewer is drawn. Regardless of the number of people or objects in a shot, one object or group of objects should be the center of interest.

Present in any well-composed picture are lines, some real, some imaginary, which lead the eye to the center of interest. In leading the eye across or through the picture, the composition itself takes on movement, and movement of this type is almost as interesting as the literal type discussed in a previous chapter. For example, imagine the classical type of picture we have seen so many times. A path or road leads away from the onlooker, and the eye automatically follows it to the background where it meets a building, a sunset, or other pertinent object. Or imagine a shot wherein a small boy in the foreground is looking up at a great statue in the background. An imaginary line connects the boy to the statue, and as the eye moves from one to the other, the onlooker gains a sense

SOME IDEAS
concerning
COMPOSITION

Don't

Do

Apply the Rule of Thirds.

Include only the area necessary to tell your story.

Balance the frame.

Try to "frame" your long shots.

Compose the shot in depth.

of movement. These lines, which we might call "lines of force," are existent in almost every well-composed picture; usually in the most interesting shots, if the lines are straight, they travel diagonally across the frame, or if curved, they follow a graceful S across the frame from foreground to background.

One of the most elementary, and most often violated, principles of composition is the principle of filling the frame. No more area should be included in the picture than is necessary to tell the story. This does not mean, of course, that every scene should be a close-up and that long shots are poor composition. It does mean, however, that we should show just what we desire and no more, that the edges must contribute to the center portions of the picture, that the subject should not appear to rattle around in the frame. Sometimes, in long shots, it is desirable to use branches, logs, or some other prop to form a natural frame. Such a frame, appearing in the foreground, gives the picture depth, life, and consequent interest.

The various principles and rules of good composition are, at best, a substitute for good taste and an intelligent eye. Just like music or a piece of poetry, a picture must have form, balance, and rhythm. Also just like music and poetry, the composition of various pictures may differ in style. It may be a Bach or a Gershwin, a Wordsworth or a Lindsay. It may adhere to all the rules or it may adhere to no rules, but if it achieves its objective, whether that be to annoy or to satisfy, it is good composition.

THE LENS AND COMPOSITION

The tool used by the cameraman to gain the desired composition is the lens. Frequently, the composition seen by the normal eye's perspective is far from desirable, but altering this perspective by use of a wide angle or long focal-length lens will achieve startling results.

The most frequent problem is the relationship in size between foreground and background objects or subjects. Suppose our center of interest is a building, and we wish to frame it by means of trees and branches in the foreground. The normal eye perspective of the two-inch lens, when placed far enough away to include the tree trunks and branches, records the building as too far away—too small in relation to the foreground. However, if we move the camera still farther away, use a three-inch lens, and get the same composition on the trees and branches, we will find the building to be much closer and larger in relation to the trees. The fact that the foreground framing may be in soft focus offers no problem as long as it is not overly blurred; rather it aids in leading the eye to the sharp center of attraction. If the foreground is too far out of focus, it is often feasible to take the light off it and make it appear almost as a silhouette.

The general rule in controlling the comparative sizes of foreground and background objects is: the shorter the focal length of the lens, the smaller are the background objects in relation to the foreground; and vice versa, the longer the focal length of the lens, the larger will be background objects in relation to the foreground.

LIGHTING

Like composition and lenses, lighting is the subject of many volumes, and will be the subject of many more in the future. Those who have a particular interest in any of these subjects should consult some of the many books available. It is not our purpose to discuss lighting techniques and practices, for they belong in the technical field of the cameraman. Rather, we merely wish to introduce some of the terms and procedures with which the director should be familiar.

To the uninitiated onlooker, a motion picture set appears like a maze of lights—little lights and big lights, barrel-shaped spotlights standing on pipelike stands, intensely strong searchlight affairs set high in the air, flat dishpan-like contraptions that glow with a soft even light, rows of spotlights hanging from the "grids" over the set, and small "inkies" not much stronger than a flashlight. It seems as if the cameraman has entirely surrounded the action with lights which shine haphazardly with little rhyme or reason, and yet we know that the finished result could not come to life on the screen without a very definite plan and execution.

All the light directed upon a given subject from the many and various sources falls into one of three general categories. There is the *key light*. That is the primary light source of the scene. If the scene is shot to simulate an exterior, the key light is a very strong light used to simulate the sun. It is usually placed in front of the subject but at an angle to the camera so as to throw well-defined shadows. In black-and-white photography it is the shadows and highlights that make the picture; thus, the placement of the key light is of primary importance.

The *fill light* is a softer light coming from the front and sides and which fills in the shadows thrown by the key light. If a fill light is not used, the shadows become almost a jet black rather than the pleasing grays which do not obliterate details.

The *back light* is placed high and to the rear so that it casts a halo of light on the edges of the subject. It "pulls" the subject out from the background and gives depth to the picture.

The cameraman's problem is to so balance these lights that the over-all picture is evenly illuminated: the highlights not washed out and with detail in the shadows. Since motion picture film does not have nearly the latitude of the human eye, effective lighting demands some very precise work. The cameraman's individual technique is composed of the method or methods he uses to balance his lights; whether the scene is a face close-up of one actor or a long shot of a ballroom with hundreds of dancing couples, his technique is the same. In the close-up it is only more exacting, and in the long shot it is repeated many times because of the number of subjects and their movements.

The studio lights which are used on an interior set are generally classified as *broads* or *spots*. A broad is a panlike light which is covered with etched, translucent glass, and which gives a soft, over-all illumination. It is often used to supply a fill light. A spot is a barrel-shaped affair which rifles a hard beam of light on any spe-

The "Baby"

The "Broad"

The "Senior"

The 225 arc light known as "The Brute"

A few of the lights used on a motion picture set.

71

cific point. Spots are broken down into *fives*, *deuces*, *seven-fifties*, and *inkies*. A five is a 5,000-watt light, a deuce a 2,000-watt light, a seven-fifty a 750-watt light, and an inkie a very small spotlight. A five is also sometimes referred to as a *senior*, a deuce as a *junior*, and a seven-fifty as a *baby*.

If the shot is to simulate an exterior set, there may also be one or more *arcs*. An arc is a carbon arc spotlight which supplies a very brilliant light that takes the place of sunlight.

The cameraman has several methods at his disposal to control the intensity of the lights. With spots he can control it by means of a knob on the back of the light which focuses the beam from a very narrow, intense shaft to a broad light of much lesser intensity. He can also put in front of the light a net or *scrim* which cuts down its brilliance. Nets and scrims are also used on broads, but these lights have no such interior control as do spots. The cameraman moves the broad away or toward the subject to control its intensity.

To mask off light where it is not wanted, the cameraman uses a *gobo*. A gobo is a black piece of thin plywood which is usually mounted on a *century stand*. A century stand is an upright pipe supplied with adjustable arms and clamps.

When shooting exterior scenes on location, the cameraman may rely on the sun entirely, or he may use studio lights to supply back and fill lighting. Either way, he will probably supplement the illumination with reflectors, large rectangular pieces of plywood covered with silver paper.

In the studio, the director can ask his cameraman to shoot in practically any direction, and the cameraman will light the scene to suit. However, when shooting on location, the director must consider the sun in his plans. Normally, the sun should shine on the scene at about a 45-degree angle with the camera axis. If the sun is shining directly over the shoulder of the cameraman, the scene will lack shadows and become flat. If the sun is behind the scene, shining toward the camera, the subjects will be covered with their own shadows and be almost silhouettes. This situation, in a close-up, is not disastrous because reflectors can be used to light

(U.S. Army Photo)

When shooting exteriors, the cameraman can cut down the intensity of direct sunlight with net-like affairs called scrims, and he can fill in the deep shadows by use of reflectors. This picture was taken on a location of *No Place Like Home*, an army short subject directed by the author.

up the face; indeed, this type of close-up is often better than that with the sun striking directly on the face. When shooting a long shot, however, it would be impossible to fill in the scene with reflected light or even the illumination of studio lights.

Since the sun moves across the sky, some scenes are morning shots, some are afternoon shots, and some can be shot at either time. There are many other factors which influence exterior shooting, and inasmuch as the cameraman is charged with putting the scene on film, he should, whenever possible, be consulted in advance about the angles planned and their scheduling.

NIGHT EFFECTS

Interior night effects constitute a specialized lighting problem which does not concern the director too much nor offer him any particular problems. Exterior night effects, however, must be shot under certain light conditions of which the director should be aware.

Realistic night scenes can be filmed during the hours of dusk or dawn, but such a procedure offers very little production time and is, therefore, not generally practiced except for isolated scenes. Some night scenes, where artificial light is in abundance and is so intended to appear, are actually filmed at night. The most common procedure, however, is to shoot the scenes in brilliant sunshine.

In its simplest terms, day-for-night shooting, as it is called, involves the use of a red filter and the underexposure of the film. Certain light conditions must be met: the scene should be in cross-light—the sun shining at right angles to the camera axis—and there should be a brilliant sun with a clear blue sky without haze or clouds. The red filter turns the sky-blue into a dark gray or black, but it also records clouds or overcast as an extreme white. Cross-light is desirable, because the long black shadows it gives heighten the night effect.

In choosing exterior locations for night effects, the director looks for shadows and cross-light for as much of the shooting day as possible.

CAMERA MOVEMENT

The intelligent use of movement is one of the basic techniques by which the director secures audience interest. However, unless movement is planned with the job of the camera operator in mind, camera movement can be the cause of many director-cameraman controversies and, indeed, the cause of many ruined takes. The director must remember that the more the camera must pan and tilt, the more chance there is for error and consequent reshooting of the scene. He must remember, too, that it is even more difficult to pan and tilt while on a moving dolly and that the constant changing of focus required offers still another chance for error. Of course, these are difficulties to be overcome and not reasons for the elimination of camera movement, for without it most films would be drab affairs. The director must find the most simple method of securing the desired result. He must realize that there is a hard way and an easy way to secure almost every moving effect, and that nothing exasperates a skilled technician more than being forced to accomplish something the hard way.

Let us consider the focus problem. During a moving shot, the center of interest must be constantly in focus, every move predetermined, and the camera-subject distance measured at each point. Then, during the take, an assistant cameraman must turn the focus ring or the lens itself so that the focus changes with the movement. Now, as we know, within certain limits, the longer the focal length of the lens, the smaller and more "critical" is the depth of field. Therefore, to ease the focus problem, the director should plan his scenes so as to take advantage of the wide angle lenses.

Another advantage of the wide angle lens is the way in which it accents movement. Since the perspective through the wide angle lens increases the apparent distance from foreground to background, a subject moving toward or away from the camera appears to move faster than it actually does. This type of movement is more pleasing, as we know, than is movement directly across the screen, and with the wide angle lens we can make it even more pleasing.

One of the disadvantages of this type of lens, however, is the distortion which may result during a pan. Sometimes, with an extremely wide angle lens, vertical straight lines have a tendency to bow or bend. Ordinarily, during a static shot, this is not noticeable, but during a pan, the lines can sometimes be observed bending as they move near the edges of the screen toward and away from the center.

In movement toward a close-up, the focus problem is much more difficult than when movement is receding from the close-up. The

The Theory of the EXPANDING AND CONTRACTING TRIANGLE

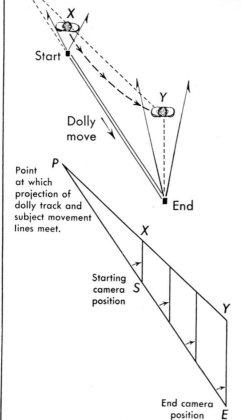

Start

X

Y

Dolly move

Point at which projection of dolly track and subject movement lines meet.

End

P

X

Starting camera position

S

Y

End camera position

E

An ideal situation, not too often possible. But if we strive to apply it, we'll make the operator's job easier, and the movement smoother.

Since:
$$\angle PSX = \angle PEY$$
and the intermediate angles are equal, the camera does not need to pan.

depth of field becomes increasingly small as we move closer to the camera; it increases as we move away. When the movement is away from the subject, the closer focus can be preset before the shot begins and the most precise work is completed. If the movement is toward the subject, the critical focus change must be accomplished during the move.

Moving camera scenes can be made from either the dolly or the boom. The dolly fixes the height of the camera and enables it to travel only in a straight line along the tracks. It is possible to swing the arm of the dolly during a scene, but this is not recommended and is very seldom done. The camera boom, however, allows camera movement in any direction. Like the dolly, the boom can be moved forward and backward in a straight line, but in addition the long arm of the boom is constructed for easy swinging up and down and from side to side during the move. This enables the camera to travel along three planes or in a three-dimensional arc.

In spite of its versatility, the boom is rather restricted in use because of the skill necessary to operate the camera and the number of stagehands needed to move the boom and swing its arm. Too, the boom is a very expensive item of equipment which many studios do not have and which takes considerable stage space. These factors limit its use to a few scenes in the higher budget pictures.

To use the dolly properly, the director should understand the principle of what I call the expanding and contracting triangle. One side of the triangle is the dolly track, another side the path of the subject movement, and the third side an imaginary line from the camera to the subject at any point during the shot. The theory can be applied in almost any dolly scene in which the subject movement and camera movement are not parallel.

Visualize a plan view for a contemplated dolly shot. Draw a line for the dolly tracks, a line connecting the camera and the subject at their farthest points, and a line for the path of the subject. (If the subject moves in a curve, connect the starting and stopping positions with a straight line.) If we now extend the dolly-track and subject-movement lines until they meet, we will have a triangle.

If we so pace the movement of both subject and dolly that the angle between the dolly-track line and the camera-subject line remains the same throughout the scene, we have planned a dolly scene in which the camera need not pan except for minor corrections in composition. Of course, it is not always possible to so plan a scene; many other factors must be considered, but the director will find that if he understands the theory of the expanding and contracting triangle, and if he applies it where he is able, the number of NG ("no good") takes will diminish considerably.

In practice, this theory can be applied as follows: suppose we plan to move the subject from point X to point Y as the camera moves from a close-up to a medium shot. Point X is fixed because it is in front of a door through which the subject has just entered. Point Y is in a given general area which we shall call area Y until point Y is definitely established.

First, have the subject stand at point X and, with the detachable view-finder removed from the camera, frame the subject into the desired close-up. Place a chalk mark on the floor at your feet. It marks the starting camera position.

Now, have the subject stand in the center of area Y. Again use the view-finder to frame the subject into the desired medium shot. As you do this, take such a position that you are looking through the finder on a line approximately parallel to the direction you were looking when you spotted the subject at point X. You will have to move about and experiment a bit to do this, for you are trying to satisfy two conditions: desirable composition and a line of sight parallel to your original line of sight. When you find the proper spot, mark it on the floor at your feet as the end camera position. Now, lay the dolly track connecting the two camera positions you have marked on the floor. After the track has been laid and the dolly is on it, place the camera over your first chalk mark and have your subject stand at point X. Pan and tilt and adjust the height of the camera to get the desired composition for the close-up, and then, *without moving from the desired composition, lock off the pan gear.*

Next, push the dolly back until the camera is over the second chalk mark and have the subject move to the center of area Y. Look through the camera and, without disturbing the pan gear, *have the subject move* so as to get into the desired composition at the end of the shot. Place a mark on the floor at his feet. *That mark is point Y.* The shot is now set up.

During execution, it is important that the camera start when the subject starts and stop when the subject stops. One moves as the other moves, and the operator will find that he has practically no panning during the scene and that his chance for error is relatively small. Not only is such a scene easier to execute than one requiring considerable panning, but it is frequently much smoother on the screen.

Sometimes, however, considerable panning, tilting, and dolly movement are necessary to get the desired effect. The director is usually striving for an effect of maximum subject movement with minimum camera movement, but such a scene sometimes involves much more camera movement than is evident on the screen. When it becomes evident that a scene requiring considerable camera movement is necessary, the director must not forget, in his desire to ease the work of the camera crew, that, regardless of the difficulties involved, they will all be forgotten if the resulting scene is good. Any camera operator worth his salt will take the scene in stride. The director must only decide, economically and artistically, the answer to "Is it worth it?"

SPECIAL EFFECTS

In the larger, well-organized studios there are usually one or more departments which handle special-effects photography. Special effects are the scenes which do not come within the usual scope of the production cameraman's work and which should be handled by specialists apart from regular production.

The *insert* is one type of special effect which is usually handled by a separate department after the production shooting is finished.

As extreme close-ups of some pertinent object or action, inserts are very critical in focus, composition, and lighting, and are often quite time-consuming to make. To spend time on them while a large crew and expensive cast stand about on the set would be extremely uneconomical.

Miniatures are a form of special effects in which a full-sized set is reconstructed in model size to perfect scale. The train wreck, the blowing up of the bridge, the burning building—all too expensive to produce full scale—are filmed by means of finely detailed models and techniques which are of little concern to the director.

Matte shots are used when part of the scene is a full-sized set and part is a shot of a miniature, a piece of art work, or some entirely different landscape. The two scenes are combined by optical printing. An example of a matte shot might be a shot of a large set on an interior stage which is not built high enough to include the sky and distant background mountains. The long shots are filmed as is normally done except that the camera shoots over the top of the set. Later, the film is turned over to experts who put in the sky and distant mountains in place of the area over the top of the set.

THE PROCESS SCREEN

Process screen, or *background projection* as it is sometimes called, is the motion picture production method of bringing locations to the studio. The desired background for a given scene is photographed on location. Back in the studio, this background is projected upon a translucent screen so that it appears on the side of the screen opposite to the projector. In front of the screen (the side opposite to the projector) the actors perform their roles, and both actors and background are photographed by the production camera. The result, on the theater screen, is a scene in which the actors apparently act their roles on the location at which the background was filmed.

The use of the process screen has several distinct advantages.

A process screen has a picture of battle-torn Europe projected through it.

An army jeep is placed in the foreground.

After the actors are in position, we see the scene as the movie or television audience will see it.

(U.S. Army Photos)

Background projection is the motion picture production method of bringing locations to the studio.

To transport an entire production crew, together with actors, to a location far from the studio, costs many thousands of dollars. This cost may be justified if a large portion of the film is to be shot on location, but, for only a few scenes, it is usually much less expensive to send a process camera crew to the location to film the background and then actually shoot the scene in the studio by means of the process screen. In addition to its use for economic reasons, the process screen can be used to produce certain scenes which might otherwise be impossible to shoot. Dialogue scenes involving cumbersome sound equipment in moving automobiles or trains where the passing exterior is visible, would be practically impossible to shoot without the process screen.

Process work also has several disadvantages which must likewise be considered. The long throw of the projector requires considerable stage space, and unless a crew is especially trained for the work and does nothing else, process work is not as fast as ordinary production. Thus, in large studios which are geared to use it constantly, the process screen will represent a distinct saving, but in smaller organizations which use it rather infrequently, it can be somewhat slow and expensive.

Although the principle of rear projection is comparatively simple, the execution is quite exacting. Many of the details concern the camera crew only, but many others should be understood by the director as well.

Scenes must be planned completely and almost to the last detail before even the backgrounds are shot, and once those backgrounds are on film, the director cannot change his planned camera angles. All the pertinent details of the camera set-up for shooting the background must be duplicated in the studio camera set-up. The height of the camera from the ground, the deviation from the horizontal, and the focal length of the lens must be the same on both the background and the studio camera. Furthermore, in the studio, the shooting axis of the projector and the studio camera must be along the same line. If the studio camera is not set up the same as the background camera, the result may be an incongruous per-

A FEW PRINCIPLES
of
THE PROCESS SCREEN

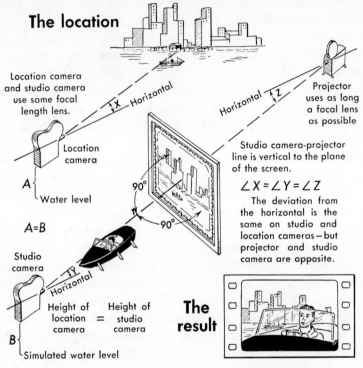

The location

Location camera and studio camera use same focal length lens.

Location camera

A { Water level

A=B

Studio camera

Horizontal X

90°

90°

Horizontal Y

Horizontal Z

Projector uses as long a focal lens as possible

Studio camera-projector line is vertical to the plane of the screen.

$$\angle X = \angle Y = \angle Z$$

The deviation from the horizontal is the same on studio and location cameras — but projector and studio camera are opposite.

Height of location camera = Height of studio camera

The result

B { Simulated water level

In practice, however, it is possible to cheat from these optimum conditions. But the process cameramen, not the director, should decide how much it is possible to cheat.

spective, and if the studio camera and the projector do not shoot along the same axis, the exposure on the background will be uneven, too dark on one side, too light on the other.

Although the exact focal lengths of the lenses need not be the same for both background and studio cameras, the variance should be very small. For example, the background camera may use a 35mm. lens and the studio camera a 40mm., but if one camera were to use a 50mm. and the other a 35mm. lens, the perspective of background and foreground would be quite different and the scene distorted.

Pan shots are to be avoided with process work. If the effect of a short pan is necessary, it is better to make a short truck shot diagonally to the screen with the studio camera axis always parallel to the projector axis.

When it is necessary to show the ground upon which the actors are standing, it is also necessary to construct a foreground piece. If, on the other hand, the scene is only a waist close-up, a foreground piece may not be necessary. Any foliage or construction between the actors and the camera must be present in the studio. The process screen shows only the background.

In practice, the general procedure on location is to set up the background camera just as in an actual shooting of the scene. Doubles are sometimes used to line up the shot. After the composition is set, the camera is clamped down on the tripod to make sure there is no vibration. Then all the pertinent data are recorded: the height of the camera, its deviation from the horizontal, the distance to the doubles, and the focal length of the lens. The doubles are then removed, and the background is filmed. Back in the studio, the reverse procedure is used in lining up the scene with the actors to play the parts.

Process work is very exacting, and it cannot be hurried. However, if properly done it can reduce expenses considerably and produce effects otherwise impossible to attain. If the director understands the work and plans his scenes accordingly, the jobs of both background cameraman and studio cameraman will be much easier.

THE CAMERAMAN AND THE DIRECTOR

The relationship between the cameraman and the director can often mean the difference between a good film and a mediocre film, a film over the budget and a film under the budget. While each has his own job, many decisions must be arrived at mutually. Filters, emulsions, processing, and methods of lighting are strictly the concern of the cameraman; editing and acting are strictly the concern of the director. However, composition, movement, at times the lens, and the ultimate lighting effect are phases in which both are vitally interested: the cameraman because they are his to execute, the director whenever they concern the editorial pattern and mood of the scene.

Neither the director nor the cameraman can afford to be touchy as to his prerogatives, and neither should become dictatorial. They must work their problems out together, mutually respecting each other and each other's desire for a finer product. The producer or studio executive who, when making assignments, considers the personalities of his directors and cameramen is also considering his pocketbook and the worth of the finished film.

CHAPTER SIX

ACTORS AND ACTIONS

The mere appreciation of technique is not complimentary to a film, but the vivid recollection of a living experience is indeed a high tribute. Technique, whether it be the cameraman's, the director's, or the actor's, is used only to accomplish a purpose. If the technique is apparent, the purpose is not accomplished. If the technique passes unnoticed in the flush of aroused emotions, the purpose *is* accomplished.

Nowhere can technique be more apparent than in acting, and nowhere is it more offensive. For this reason, the actor ranks alongside the writer in importance. If the scenario is well written and if the film is well acted, the photographic quality, the sound, and even the visual continuity may be second-rate without necessarily resulting in a poor film. However, if both the scenario and the acting are weak, nothing the director or his technicians can do will save the picture.

All too often the director has little control over his scenario. Over his actors, though, his control is almost absolute. He has a major hand in selecting them, and he directly guides and controls their performances. Therefore, the director must know the actor's problems; he must recognize convincing acting, and he must spot instantly any evidence of "technique" or overacting.

As the camera rolls and he watches the scene unfold, the director's taste must serve as the representative of all the audiences who will ever see the film.

THE ACTOR'S PROBLEM

Just as there are different media of entertainment and communication, so are there different styles of acting. The radio, where the actor is heard but not seen, demands an emphasis on the voice. The stage, where the actor is seen and heard from a distance, demands a projection, or overemphasis, of both voice and actions. Motion pictures and television, where the actor is often seen and heard as intimately as in real life, demand the restraint of both voice and action.

When performing for the screen, the actor must be utterly and completely natural. Techniques of projecting both body movements and voice which are necessary to portray life on the stage, become, on the screen, mere displays of technique. For this reason, even the finest stage actors sometimes have difficulty accustoming themselves to the screen.

On the stage, the actor performs the story in a single unit—from the beginning to the end. He can build as he goes along. He can judge the reaction of his audience. To this audience, seated many yards from him, he projects his emotions by means of finely developed techniques. His whisper becomes a loud, forceful hiss—a "stage whisper." His casual speech becomes louder, more distinct, than normal conversation. Movements are exaggerated. Downcast eyes become drooping shoulders. Raised eyebrows become a tilting head. The motion of a finger becomes the swinging of an arm. Enunciation becomes too distinct, too precise. But the audience, because of its distance from him, sees and hears a normal whisper, downcast eyes, and raised eyebrows. Voices seem casual, movements seem normal. The actor, by means of overt actions, projects living experience.

The difference between stage acting and screen acting is like performing for the opposite ends of a telescope. The screen is a magnifier. The image of the actor's nose may be five feet long, his eyes, three feet apart. The audience sees him, at times, as if they were face to face with him in a tiny room. They hear his voice as it really is; they see more than the twitch of an eyelid or the raising of a brow. The brutality of film reflects emotions which come from within the actor. He becomes real, not a figure on a stage. The actor must not "act." He must live. He must forget technique as he attempts to feel the emotions of his part and then conceal them— just as man everywhere feels his sorrows, triumphs, and lost hopes, but often tries to hide his reactions from his fellow men.

In his book, *The Art of The Motion Picture*, Jean Benoit-Levy, the great French director, wrote, "It may be said that a screen player's ambition should be to equal the unconscious talent of natural actors, since in the last analysis he will not achieve the fullest development of his art until he is able to express the emotions he himself experiences. His talent will then enable him to concentrate on not letting professional technique distort the unconscious reactions of his personality, which he will transmit through the delicate range of his feelings." *

The actors who are able to build a personality other than their own into a screen character are rare indeed. A certain few of our great actors of the past two decades have been able to play effectively many and varied personalities for the screen, but the great majority of even competent actors are limited to reflecting their own personalities in a given situation. Reactions of an actor to the situation may vary just as do our own from day to day, but only one personality comes through—his own!

On the stage, it is quite different. There, the actor need not weather the terrible scrutiny of the telltale close-up, and an accomplished actor is able to play many different personalities.

Mechanical limitations of motion picture production add further

---

* From *The Art of the Motion Picture* by Jean Benoit-Levy; copyright 1946 by Jean Benoit-Levy; reprinted by permission of Coward-McCann, Inc.

to the screen actor's difficulties. Scenes are seldom shot in the order of their appearance. Thus, he cannot build to the audience reaction of the stage. The unity of his performance must be mental. He must know where he is going. He must have arrived at the end before he begins. He must depend far more on his director than need his stage counterpart.

Technical requirements hinder the screen actor at every hand. He must remember to match his actions so that the film can be cut. He must tilt his head a certain way to avoid a given light. When there is camera movement, he must time his actions exactly so that the grips, the camera operator, and the other actors may be able to time their movements. The screen actor must avoid unexpected motions which might throw the picture out of composition; he must walk and stop within certain prescribed limits, and he must hold his voice within certain volume levels so that it may be properly recorded. And with all this, he must be completely natural in his performance!

The professional actor, because of the nature of his work, is often a spirited, highly sensitive individual. His emotions are attuned to the emotions of others, and his actions and reactions reflect theirs just as surely as a mirror reflects a physical appearance. And yet, categorically, he is often indifferent to the feelings of others. Impatient with the prosaic technical problems that beset motion pictures, he is interested only in the reactions to his performance. He is a mimic, an exhibitionist. Beyond these things, however, he varies just as do people in all other walks of life. He may be generous or selfish, kind or vicious, quiet or noisy, intelligent or stupid.

This complex individual, the professional actor, is the person whom the director must guide, influence, and compel to be completely natural. He is the person upon whom the director must depend to bring life to the screen.

The director's relationship with the actor runs through two phases. The first phase, the selection of particular actors for particular parts, is known as casting. The second phase takes place after casting. It is the period before and during production when the director must help those actors who have been selected to bring their parts to life.

CASTING PROCEDURES

The administrative procedures in casting vary according to the producing set-up, the film, the geographical location, and the producer-director relationship. Furthermore, the parts which the actors fill are generally classified as *leads, supporting players, bit parts,* and *extras.*

The leads are those characters upon whom the foundation of the story rests. Appearing in the majority of scenes, a lead takes part in most of the production, and his interpretation of his part greatly influences the director's handling of the story. Quite often there are two leads, a male and a female. Generally billed as name stars in theatrical films, they are often the advertising wedge used to sell the film.

Supporting players are those members of the cast who appear somewhat frequently throughout the film, but who are not, story-wise, important enough to be classified as leads. Supporting the action of the leads, they are the relations, friends, or enemies of the protagonist.

Bit players appear once or twice in a given picture, say a few words of dialogue or perform a significant bit of action, and then disappear. Acting as the hotel clerk who registers the lead, the waiter who serves him in the night club, or the taxi driver who drives him to the station, the bit player must perform his part naturally and convincingly, and yet work in a film for, at most, only a few days.

Extras are those players who make up the human movement in the foreground and background of the various scenes. Known, too, as "atmosphere," they are the patrons of the hotel or night club, the street passers-by, the soldiers of the attacking body of troops, the members of the shouting mob. Extras are classified according to the particular work they do. In fact, the minimum wage contract of the Screen Extras' Guild lists some fifteen major classifications, including riders, singers, drivers, dancers, and doubles.

In Hollywood, where organization and typing are at their best or worst depending upon the viewpoint, actors are classified and trained only for the particular type of acting they do. They have a Screen Actors' Guild and a Screen Extras' Guild, and at one time, the Screen Actors' Guild issued various types of cards depending upon the work of the member.

It is interesting to note, in this connection, that many actors would refuse to step into another class even though the pay might be better. To be raised to the level of a lead, with a possibly short box-office life, might spoil the character actor's value as a supporting player. Often the extra refuses other work, although the ranks of Hollywood extras are filled with those who were once great stars, or who, as beginners, are preparing, working, and dreaming of their "big chance."

The situation varies somewhat in other geographical locations. Since the New York Screen Actors Guild is associated with the west coast actors' and extras' guilds through The Associated Actors and Artists of America, there is little difference between the east coast and west coast as far as union regulations are concerned. However, the entirely different organizational setups and financial resources of the producing agencies cause certain procedural differences. In Hollywood, the studios are highly organized and have almost unlimited resources, whereas in New York, a producer is often one individual, without studio or equipment of his own, who works within a limited budget. These circumstances, in turn, often compel the Eastern actor to consider prestige of somewhat lesser importance than he would on the west coast.

Throughout all sections of the country, actors secure work through agents who function somewhat like employment agencies. However, the tie between actor and agent is much closer and bound by more definite rules than is the usual employment-agency-job-hunter relationship. In most occupations, jobs are held for years and not infrequently a lifetime. In the theatrical profession, jobs last for very short periods, perhaps a day or two, or at most a month—excluding, of course, those in "hit" plays. Thus, the actor spends much of his time job-hunting, and he is constantly changing employers.

To handle their continual job-seeking, actors normally have agents who are paid a certain percentage of the wages. Some actors have several agents, while others sign an "exclusive contract" with a particular agent. Most agents have many actors in their "stalls," and some, like the William Morris Agency, are large business organizations with hundreds of actors.

In the large west coast studios, some actors work on a contract basis with particular studios. From its ranks of these actors, the studio will fill the leads, supporting players' parts, and, to some extent, the bits. Thus, it is the dream of an actor with less prestige to secure a contract with one of the studios and acquire a regular meal ticket. Other actors in Hollywood, being in great demand and preferring the freedom of "free-lancing," work on a job-to-job basis. Elsewhere than the west coast, because of the limited resources of the producing companies, all actors work on a free-lance basis.

In Hollywood, where production often requires thousands of extras daily, there exists a Central Casting Corporation. This organization has listings of all the various and special types of free-lance actors, and it acts as a clearing house for the major studios. Each day, Central Casting receives a list from the studios of the numbers and types of extras and bits necessary for the next day's work. About five o'clock in the evening, thousands of actors call Central Casting. Those who are on the list are notified of the job, the time and place to report, the costume, type of film, and other necessary details. In addition to adding to the efficiency of the producing organizations, Central Casting has improved the lot of the professional bit and extra. Gone, now, are the tragic lines at the studio gate, and the actor today waits by the telephone.

In New York, the system is entirely different. As in Hollywood, there are agents whose livelihood depends on securing jobs for actors, but, unlike agents in Hollywood, the agents in New York also act as a sort of Central Casting. Actors are frequently registered with several agents, and producing organizations often call for actors through the agents. When the producer wishes to cast leads or supporting players, he tells the agent to send a group of eligible applicants to a casting session. At this session, the director and producer choose their actors and perhaps select a few to be given tests for the leading parts. In the case of bits and extras, the producer selects the actors, notifies them, and gives them necessary instructions.

Frequently, in New York, the producer contacts the actor directly. The method of contact varies with the situation. Procedures are not as rigid as in the more highly organized west coast systems.

In Hollywood, the scenario is often designed as a vehicle for a particular star who is under contract, and the lead is thus determined before the scenario is even written or the director suggested. In this case, it may be the actor who helps select the director rather than vice versa. On the other hand, the scenario may be written with several stars in mind for the lead, and the producer will then consult his prospective director before making a final decision.

Usually the director will have a major hand in selecting all the leads, supporting players, and bits, if he so desires, but he must be prepared for varying situations such as those in which the scenario was written for several leads, in which the producer has already selected leads and some supporting players, or in which relations and favorites of studio executives or sponsors are earmarked for certain parts. Of course, the prestige of the individual director has great influence on the method used.

BALANCING THE CAST

In dramatic circles, one will frequently hear the phrases "casting to type" or "casting against type."

Casting to type refers to casting in conformity with certain patterns of appearances and actions. These patterns type professions and occupations with specific attributes. For example, bank clerks are portrayed as meek, bald, and physically delicate, and gangsters as ugly, characterized by crooked noses, and speaking in a marked Brooklyn dialect. Through a lifetime of watching films cast to this formula, the American public has grown to expect types, and many directors feel that this is a compelling reason to continue type casting. Other directors have violated the formula and have come up with prize-winning films.

Casting against type refers to the deliberate violation of the type-casting procedure. Here criminals may smoke pipes and speak with an Oxford accent, while writers may be ugly with crooked noses.

I believe that in certain short subjects the limited showing time may be an excuse for type casting. The audience has very little time in which to grasp the characters of the players. However, in the longer, more serious works, we should cast to type or against type no more than the Creator cast men into given molds so as to advertise their characters. If the film is to create a portion of life, it must look to life for its characters. The audience must react to the players as they react to acquaintances and associates. They must react individually; just as in life, no two persons have the same reaction to a third.

Individuals are highly complicated; no two are alike. Each is a unique blend of intricacies, and the director who casts to type or against type is casting to a hackneyed formula that has little basis in the life he wishes to bring to the film.

Remembering that the best actor will transmit his own personality "through the delicate range of his feelings," it becomes the director's job to analyze the personalities—not physical appearances —of the characters he wishes to portray in his film. Next, for each part, he should attempt to secure several applicants whose personalities most coincide with that part. Then, and only then, should he balance the physical features of his actors so that in the final selection of his cast he will have people of such varied appearances that the audience can in no way mistake one character for any other.

In balancing his cast, it is best if the director starts with his leads. The others should be matched to these, not these to the others. Once the leads are selected, the director goes on to supporting players. Their physical characteristics are matched against those of the leads and other supporting players. The director will strive to gain contrasts in appearance, and throughout the casting he will continually ask himself about each actor, "Is this person a natural actor or merely a trained exhibitionist? Does this person's personality suit the personality of the part?"

AMATEUR ACTORS

A few years ago a trend developed among theatrical studios producing so-called documentary films. Patterned somewhat after the successful documentaries of Flaherty, Lorenz, and others, but using a plot story, these films often used amateurs for bit and extra parts. On location away from the studio, and needing a policeman or gas station attendant, the director secured a policeman or gas station attendant whose natural aptitude enabled him to play the part.

For years, educational and industrial producers have followed this idea and reserved only the leads for trained professional actors. Sometimes even the lead may be entrusted to a talented amateur.

At one time, I directed an army training film with completely live-sound* dialogue and story plot, and I used not a single professional actor. The result was a closeness to reality that even the very best actors would have found difficulty in securing. Furthermore, the professionals' performance might have conveyed a dramatic interpretation entirely out of place in that type of film.

Although often resented by the professional, the use of nonprofessionals should serve as a spur rather than as a subject of dissension and union regulations. The professional actor should not concentrate on an academic approach to the theater, but should try to know life in many of its facets, and for a time take jobs

* See definition of live sound, p. 104.

unrelated to films, television, and the theater. His experience should be broad and his insight keen. When playing a scene, he must forget technique and live the part. Only when he is capable of becoming a policeman off the screen can he be truly convincing as a policeman on the screen.

During World War II many of our finest professional actors were forced into lines of work utterly foreign to films. With but few exceptions they proved that their abilities as natural actors stemmed from a wealth of understanding and talent in other lines. One of the best known was Jimmy Stewart, who progressed from lowly enlisted man to full colonel. And he did it on his own merits! The truly natural actor, professional or amateur, has abilities and interests which go far beyond mere acting.

The natural amateur is untrained in techniques, voice control, enunciation, and gestures, and is thus unhindered by the very stock in trade which trips so many professionals. The natural amateur, if he is properly cast and directed, is often incapable of giving any other than a living performance. However, in the proper selection and direction of an amateur, the director has problems which are far more complicated than those of handling professionals. Knowing the tricks of his trade, the professional can often get by with inadequate direction, but without proper handling even the best amateur is lost.

In selecting and casting the amateur, the director must have a selective range much greater than when casting professionals. Many persons have a reserve, a personality shyness, which causes them to freeze and become completely unnatural when they become the center of attraction. The extreme sincerity of others interferes with their speaking lines of dialogue convincingly. No director can obtain a natural performance from such people, and he must immediately eliminate them as possibilities. Only one in fifty persons is a natural actor. The ability seems to cross all lines of mental attainment and social position. The great documentary directors report that simple savages often have amazing abilities. In our own social world, the liars and the confidence men, who get by with their wits, are often excellent natural actors. Witness the early 1951 Senate crime investigation telecasts!

Children are frequently the best natural actors. The next best are the uninhibited, worry-free individuals whose happy outlook on life is that of a child. To choose those few from the many is often the problem of the documentary, educational, or industrial director.

BACKGROUND ACTION

Background and foreground action is the movement of people behind and in front of the central actors in a scene. Performed by extras, who create "atmosphere," it lends realism to the street, the rail station, and the café.

In addition to being essential for providing realism, background foreground action also offers another means to guide the eyes of the audience, to establish and hold a given tempo, and to add to a given mood.

The pattern of background action should generally move toward the portion of the screen occupied by the central character. Furthermore, the tempo and pace should be in keeping with the emotional experience for which the director is striving. This does not mean, of course, that all extras should move in the same direction at the same pace. It does mean, however, that the predominant movement should be in a predetermined direction at a predetermined pace. It should, with the other visual techniques, add to the emotional patterns which make up the film.

Each person in the background or foreground movement should have a purpose. Simply to walk down the street is not sufficient. To stop at a store window, contemplate it a moment, and then enter the store is everyday behavior with a purpose. Bits of business which characterize the accomplished lead and supporting player must not be neglected by the extra. They may not be consciously seen by the audience, but they will be missed if omitted.

Life goes on, and every person in the scene has a story of his own to tell.

HANDLING THE ACTOR

Handling the actor is unique to each director and to his personality. Tactics which work for one director would merely boomerang for another. The problem is a particular one, too, with each actor. The actor is an individual, not a type, and he must be studied to see how he can best be handled. Thus, between each director and actor there is a different relationship. It is up to the director to develop that association which will result in the actor's best performance.

Although relationships vary widely, depending upon the personalities of both director and actor, one basic factor remains the same. That is the director's consideration for the actor as an individual. While some directors treat their players as if they were trained cattle performing in borrowed costumes, the most successful directors respect their actors as individuals, as trained craftsmen, and as artists. The sullen anger or dissatisfaction of a cameraman, sound man, or grip may not reflect too greatly on the finished product, but the slightest influence upon the actor's emotions is instantly reflected on the screen.

Thus, a great deal of the director's efforts are extended toward guiding the emotions of his actors. Men like Ford and Huston invite their casts for long visits to their homes. They become intimately acquainted with them. They play cards, swim, ride, and chat so that the bonds between them become stronger and stronger. Often they rehearse long before a set is built, a camera turned. Then, when production actually begins, the strong actor-director relationship bears the fruit—the films—for which these men are famous.

Conditions of work, however, prevent most directors from establishing so strong a bond. But that is no reason why understanding and consideration cannot be present. A very fine character actress once told me that "handling the actor is like riding a beautiful, spirited horse." The analogy is a good one. The director's taste constitutes his reins, his tongue his spurs, and his manner his adept horsemanship. The director decides the path and whether the ride shall be a gallop, a trot, or a canter. But, as a true lover of horses, he uses no whip, and both he and the horse know where they are going.

The good director limits his actors only by the confines of pictorial movement and by his own good taste and judgment. In order that camera and subject movement may have a unity of purpose, the director must dictate certain movements and actions, and because only the director visualizes the future film in its entirety, his judgment must be final. But the director must not take advantage of this situation. He should seldom, if ever, expect his actors to mimic him. Regardless of how fine an actor the director may be, a film in which he, himself, plays all the parts is apt to be a drab affair. His actors should reflect their own personalities, their own emotions, not his! Thus, he should make sure they understand the situation; he should tell them what is wanted, but never how to do it. The actor who requires such instruction is, indeed, not an actor, but a trained mimic, an impressionist.

Just as the player should not be asked to mimic the director, so too, he should not be required to stick to the exact words of the scenario dialogue. He should not repeat lines; he should express thoughts. He should feel free to use his own words whenever he has difficulty with the scenario lines. The burden of staying within the confines of his part should lie with the director's judgment and not with the actor's. At all costs, the actor must be natural and reflect his own personality.

The director must remember that moods are more or less contagious with people even less sensitive. In actors, however, we have highly sensitive people who deal constantly in mood and emotion, and since they look to the director for guidance, their inner feelings will become, to a certain extent, a reflection of his attitude. Thus, the director who is trying to film a peaceful, happy scene but throws his actors and crew into an emotional turmoil is defeating the very purpose he is trying to accomplish.

In their efforts to guide the emotions of their actors, some directors even go to the extent of wearing clothes appropriate to the sequence they are filming. Brilliant scarfs, bright colorful shirts, and gay, plaid sport coats become their apparel when the sequence is light and cheerful. For a heavy, dramatic sequence, they wear severely tailored dark business suits with appropriate accessories. Too, their mood reflects the job at hand. When it is comedy, they become delightfully gay individuals, full of humor and pleasant ribbing. For drama, they wear a cloak of severity. Humorless and business-like, they discourage pleasantries on the part of crew and actors.

Whatever the method, the object is to help the actor reflect his own personality in the mood and circumstance of the story. It must be done within the confines of production limitations and of the editorial and movement plan of the director.

As the director talks to the actor, he is careful not to embarrass him in front of the crew or his fellow actors. Rather than issuing loud, commanding orders from the comfort of his canvas chair, the director goes to the actor. He talks with him in a low voice and makes the actor feel that what is said is just between the two of them.

If the actor is striking a wrong chord, the director explains the situation. He tries to explore the actor's mind and change his attitude concerning the part. He may discuss a similar situation with which the actor may be more familiar. "As if" are two very valuable words for the director.

If the actor is overplaying, perhaps projecting a bit, the director doesn't destroy his confidence and build a barrier between them by telling the man he is a "ham." Perhaps the actor is primarily a stage actor and needs to be reminded of the difference between the two media. "Play it down a bit" will often do wonders.

Sometimes, depending on the personalities of the director and the actor, a little light ribbing may help. In any event, the director is careful of the feelings of his actor. Not that the performer should or expects to be pampered, but the director knows that a disgruntled or unhappy actor on the set is a disgruntled or unhappy character on the screen. Only to create an unhappy feeling within the actor should the director ever be discourteous, and such tricks should be held to a minimum.

Sometimes even the best actor will come upon a word or group of words in his dialogue which becomes a mental block. Every time he reaches it he "flubs" or forgets. This is not the time for the director to lose patience, even though he may be fighting a tight schedule. Rather, the offending dialogue may be rewritten on the set, or perhaps the director can reorganize his shooting plan a little and break the scene into several shorter scenes. Then the actor may have a chance to say the troublesome line at the beginning of the take. If neither of these alternatives is possible, the director may call a brief break and allow the actor time by himself to relax and collect himself. Chances are he'll come back on the set and go right through the scene.

It is most important for the director to maintain complete mastery of the set. Not that he maintains a militaristic domination by fear, nor that he limits the creative freedom of his crew and players, but he must remember that "no man can serve two masters." If he allows the cameraman to tell the actor how to hold his head so that the lighting will be right, the script clerk to tell the actor just how to match his actions, or the sound man to tell the actor which way to turn his head as he delivers a line, the director will soon find that the actor is torn between conflicting instructions. It is quite all right for these technicians to explain their desires in the presence or with the approval of the director, or for the director to transmit the instructions himself. In any event, the director must be aware of all requests made of the actor, and the actor must at all times feel responsible to one person only—the director.

Handling the amateur is quite similar to handling the professional actor. Both are human beings who respond to consideration and leadership. It must be remembered, however, that the professional, trained in his work and having performed for many directors, is apt to resent methods which are sometimes successful with the amateur. Occasionally, the director may have to ask the amateur to mimic him. He should never ask the professional to do so.

If the director tries to trick the professional into a given reaction, the actor is apt to resent it as a lack of consideration for his professional abilities. The amateur, on the other hand, is often awed by the complicated equipment, the methods of production, and the prestige of the director. With him, the director can use tricks and appeals which would only insult the professional.

The professional actor, because of his experience, is much quicker to understand the desires of the director, and he improves with repeated rehearsals. He is able to perform a sustained piece of acting or dialogue which would absolutely floor the nonprofessional. The amateur gives his utmost on the first rehearsals, and improvements and changes must be explained in detail rather than merely suggested.

In general, working with professionals causes less strain on director and crew, and production time is usually considerably less than with amateur talent. Only on short bits of limited action in his own element is the amateur apt to give a more convincing performance.

Whether the actor be professional or amateur, the director has a fourfold purpose: First, he must choose a natural actor whose personality fits the part; second, he must make sure the actor thoroughly understands the situation; third, he must encourage the actor to express the situation in terms of his own personality; fourth, he must constantly be on the alert for any taint of projection, of overacting, and of consequent loss in the film's realism.

CHAPTER SEVEN

ABOUT SOUND

The addition of sound to motion pictures changed the screen from a silent picture of life to life itself. As characters were given voice they became alive, and the blend of sound effects and visual action made reality complete. However, before advantage of the entirely new medium could be taken, much had to be learned.

Writers had to think in terms of a much greater scope; they had to learn about the effects of sound as well as of visual techniques upon the mind. They had to write complete dialogue rather than sketchy titles.

Editors had to learn new tricks, new methods, as audible cues replaced traditional silent editing. As for the director, almost the entire scope and character of his work became different.

The director had to become more alert, more aware of the sounds and voices of life. Instead of striving for a silent projection to compensate for the lack of voice, he had to strive, through voice and action, to create reality. Even in production matters, the director's problems increased. Procedures changed and new equipment and personnel were added to the crews. New technical problems arose, and much of the director's craft was revolutionized. Either he learned to work with the new medium, or he dropped into oblivion.

The electronics of sound and sound reproduction are of vital interest only to the trained technicians who must perform the job, but there are certain procedures and limitations which the director must understand if he is to handle his crew and secure the effects he desires.

SOUND TRACK

The first application of sound to motion pictures was secured by recording the sound on disks which ran at the same speed as did the picture projectors. Later, the sound was placed on the film itself, and today we find a *sound track* on the edge of each piece of release-print sound motion picture film.

Recorded photographically on the edge of film, which in production language is known as *track*, the sound is usually kept separate from the picture during production. The track is on one film while the picture is on another. Later, for release, track and picture are combined.

Prior to the actual release of a film, many sound tracks may be used. One track, of course, is the sound secured during shooting. Called *direct recording* or *live sound*, this track includes the dialogue and sound effects incidental to each sound scene. Sound effects which are added after shooting are on another track and are matched to the picture after editing. This track—or tracks, as there may be several—include added effects for the sound scenes and the sound effects for those scenes shot without direct recording. Other tracks are made for music and narration; and, in the final act of production, called *mixing* or *dubbing*, all tracks are run synchronously with the picture, and re-recorded on one single track. This track is then printed alongside the picture on the release print.*

DIRECT RECORDING

There are two methods of direct recording, the single system and the double system. In single-system recording, the

---

* Stereophonic sound employs four tracks on the composite—one track on each side of the sprocket holes. See p. 187.

| Picture | Track | Composite |

(From a test of Dorie Field)

During production, the picture and sound are usually recorded synchronously on separate films. In editing, additional tracks—sound effects, music, and narration—are "synced" with the picture. Finally, during dubbing, all sound tracks are recorded onto one single track which is then combined optically with the picture to form a composite.

sound-recording unit is built into the camera, and both sound and picture are recorded on the same film. In double-system recording, the recorder and the camera are two separate units which are run simultaneously by synchronous motors. The sound is recorded on one film as the picture is recorded on another.

The advantages of the single system are ease of transporting and setting up the equipment and less operating personnel. The advantages of the double system are far better sound quality and ease and flexibility in editing.

The major problem in using the single system is the inferior sound quality which renders dialogue so "mushy" that it is sometimes almost unintelligible after mixing. As any photographic amateur knows, certain types of film are designed for certain specific purposes. So-called fast film which takes an image under poor light conditions has an extremely large grain, while slower films have smaller grain. Sound-recording film has extremely fine grain, so slow that it is inappropriate for ordinary photography. Thus, when one type of film is used for both sound and photography, a compromise, under which both must suffer, is inevitable. The single system, therefore, is seldom used today except for newsreel or travel work where ease of transporting and setting up is paramount. For production work, use of the double system is universal.

Another method of recording is gaining wide use in many studios. The sound is recorded magnetically and later re-recorded photographically on film. It is then edited in the usual manner. However, it makes little difference to the director whether the sound is originally recorded on magnetic tape, magnetic film, or double-system photographic film.

During production, it is necessary that each scene of picture and corresponding track be properly marked so that the editor may match each track with its corresponding picture and place the two pieces of film in synchronization. This is accomplished by the use of a *slate* and *clapsticks*. The slate, also used in silent scenes, is merely a card or slab of wood on which are printed the number of the scene and take and other pertinent information. In silent production, the slate is merely photographed at the beginning of each scene, but for sound work, the slate has the addition of clapsticks.

Clapsticks consist of two pieces of wood, hinged together, one of which is attached to the top of the slate. When slating, the slate boy calls out the scene and take numbers and then claps together the two pieces of wood. Later, the editor can see the exact frame in which the two pieces of wood came together. On the track, he can hear the sound. By matching these two points, he can "sync" track to picture.

The direct-recording sound crew generally consists of a *mixer*, a *recordist*, and a *boom man*. The mixer, who handles the console on the set, is in charge of the crew. The recordist works with the film being run through the recorder, and is usually located in another part of the studio building or in a sound truck apart from the location set. The boom man, on the set, handles the boom, or long pole, to the end of which is attached the microphone. The director's chief contact is with the mixer, who is generally referred to as the *sound man*.

THE SOUND MAN'S PROBLEM

The major problems of the sound man are to record properly those sounds which are pertinent to the film and to eliminate those sounds which are not. It must be understood that the mechanical ear of the microphone is entirely different from the human ear through which we hear sounds. The microphone picks up every sound within its range whereas the human being masks certain sounds which he does not wish to hear.

For example: Imagine that you and a friend are in a large, crowded restaurant. As you talk to each other, you are aware only of your friend. You "tune out" the chatter of the patrons, the shuffling of feet, the scraping of chairs, and the clatter of dishes. The microphone is capable of no such "tuning-out." It is entirely mechanical, and the track would record only a confusion of voices, shuffling, and clattering. Neither the voice of your friend nor the voices of the crowd would predominate.

In film production, we call that sound which we wish to hear by its proper name, *sound*, but that which we do not wish to hear, we call *noise*. The dialogue of the actors, their footsteps, and the opening and closing of doors are sound. The offstage hum of the camera, the footsteps of the stagehand, and the rattle of the studio steam pipe are noise.

It is the job of the mixer to eliminate the noise and record the sound, to be "the human brain of the mechanical microphone." To accomplish this, he has several methods which he ordinarily uses simultaneously. The first is the elimination, by directive, of all noises on the set. The second is microphone placement. The third is his control of the level of recorded sound so that noises, being of a lower level, will go unrecorded.

The law of the motion picture studio requiring silence during sound takes is inviolable. Every time a scene must be reshot because of extraneous noise, it costs the producer from several hundred to several thousand dollars. Costs of actors, crew, and stage space mount very quickly. Thus, elaborate procedures and systems have been established to insure the utmost quiet while a scene is in progress. In spite of these precautions, however, and even when they are one hundred per cent successful, there are certain noises which no mere directive can eliminate.

There is noise inherent in the film itself. Called ground or surface noise, it may be likened to the scratch of the needle on a victrola record. The methods used to reduce ground noise are mostly technical in nature and beyond the scope of the director. However, the director must understand that generally the louder the sound, the easier it is to eliminate all noise including ground noise.

Until the development of the Mitchell BNC camera, the hum of the motion picture camera presented a problem. The older models used fiber gears and were covered with a boxlike, soundproof covering known as a blimp, but still the camera could not be placed too near the microphone. When shooting extreme close-ups, it was

usually necessary to use a lens of longer focal length, and sometimes the camera and blimp had to be covered with blankets and
other sound-deadening material. The new BNC model is built as
a unit, camera and blimp, and it is so silent that it seldom presents
the close-up problem. Sometimes, however, near the beginning or
end of a thousand-foot roll of film, the microphone will pick up
the near-empty spool as it rattles in the magazine.

An edict cannot control the airplane which flies overhead, the
distant peck of a typewriter, the crunch of the dolly as it moves,
or the hundred and one other noises of which we are not conscious
until we try to record. To eliminate them, the sound man must
use other methods. One of them, as I mentioned before, is microphone placement.

Microphones can be classified as directional and nondirectional.
As the name implies, the directional microphone records sounds
from a specific direction while discriminating against sounds from
other directions. A type of directional mike frequently used in film
production is the unidirectional mike which records sound trav-
eling from only one direction. When placed on a controlled swivel
on the end of the boom, the mike can be aimed by the boom man
in the direction of the sound's source.

In addition to aiming the mike, the boom man must swing the
boom arm so that the position of the mike is such that its pick-up
is clear and in keeping with the perspective of the scene. Of course,
the closer the mike is to the sound's source, the louder is the sound
in relation to extraneous noise. Thus, when filming a dialogue scene,
the boom swings from character to character as they talk, and the
microphone spins in its swivel as it is aimed at the actor who is
speaking. Several problems, however, complicate the work of the
boom man. While he does try to get the mike close enough to the
sound's source so that the sound will have a much higher level
than the noise, he must be careful to maintain the perspective of
the picture. We cannot shoot a long shot and have the dialogue
sound as if it were right beside us, nor can we have long-shot sound
when the scene is a close-up. Furthermore, the mike or boom can-

(U.S. Army Photo)

On one of the sets of *To Hear Again*, directed by the author, the boom man places the mike in a position such that its pick-up is clear and in keeping with the perspective of the scene. Note the old style camera blimp which was still being used in 1946, the year this film was produced.

not be seen in the picture, and the boom man must be careful that the shadows of the mike are not visible. This latter is, at times, a troublesome problem, because the cameraman often has his lights trained on the action from every possible source.

On his console on the set, the mixer has a knob which is linked to a simple rheostat. This rheostat controls the sound which is channeled from the microphone to the recorder. By means of this arrangement, known as a *pot*, the mixer controls the volume of sound to be recorded. When the sound is loud, he "closes down the pot." When the sound is soft, he "opens the pot."

When the mixer opens the pot, he allows a certain amount of noise, as well as sound, to reach the recorder. On the other hand, by closing down the pot, he can eliminate the noise which is present but presumably in smaller volume than the sound. However, in closing down the pot to eliminate noise, the mixer may lose some of the desired sound.

In addition to eliminating noise, the mixer at his console also helps to control perspective and eliminate distortion of sound. Extremely loud sounds, particularly those with a sudden impact, like a pistol shot or a woman's scream, become distorted in the electronic system if they are recorded at the same level as ordinary dialogue. Therefore, the mixer must compensate to correct such distortion and secure an over-all effect akin to the sounds as picked up by the human ear.

THE DIRECTOR'S SOUND PROBLEM

We have dwelt at some length on a semitechnical discussion of direct recording and the problems of the sound man. It is important for the director to have a general understanding of these problems, because their solution is sometimes diametrically opposed to his other needs.

The director desires the best possible sound his sound crew can give him. He also desires a completely natural performance, untouched by any taint of projection, from his actors. To secure this natural performance, particularly in intimate situations, his actors must often speak in a very subdued, low voice level. It is true that the accomplished actor can raise his volume to some extent and still maintain the illusion of intimacy, but when he reaches a certain point, his vocal characteristics change, and he projects as he would on a stage. With this projection, the actor loses the ease and naturalness of both voice and action so essential to the screen. He is now "acting," and reality is lost.

The point at which the actor can no longer raise his voice without destroying the reality of an intimate scene varies with the individual actor, his abilities and training, and the particular scene involved. The experienced director can spot it almost instantly. It is the point at which a "living" scene becomes an acted one, the point at which reality becomes a transparent illusion. All too often this point is below the minimum vocal level the sound man needs to eliminate noise. Either the technical perfection of the sound must suffer, or the reality of the scene must be lost. What can be done?

First, all possibilities of simplifying the problem of the sound man must be exhausted. Any such sequences should be foreseen before production, and the walls and floors of the set should be acoustically treated. However, if during production the problem still exists, there are other solutions.

Perhaps if the mike were closer to the actor, the mixer could get his needed voice-level without the actor raising his voice. If so, it may be that the director can tighten the composition a little so that the mike could be moved in. Perhaps the mike can be hidden within the scene. As a last resort, the scene can be *lip synced* later on. Regardless of the solution, however, it is my opinion that it is much better, up to a certain point, to sacrifice technical perfection rather than the reality of the actor's performance.

Most directors feel the same way, and the best technicians face the situation intelligently. Accomplished mixers often record at a voice-level which necessitates the recording of a small amount of noise, surface or otherwise. They know that other sound technicians may notice it, but they also know that it will pass unnoticed by the untrained ear. As part of the production team, they constantly strive for the highest technical standards, but when their own individual standards must be sacrificed for the good of the picture, they are willing to go as far as is humanly possible. Only when the need for sacrifice threatens to become so great as to dispel the illusion for the average audience do they become adamant. It is then that the director must find another solution. Occasionally, that solution is the use of *lip sync.*

LIP SYNC

At times, on exterior locations, the noises of wind, automobiles, and so on are so loud that direct recording is impossible, regardless of the actor's voice-level. At such times, the director and sound man usually decide to lip sync the sequence. In this procedure, the mixer makes what is known as a *cue track* for each scene. No attempt is made to eliminate noise; the only object of recording is to get an exact audio record of the dialogue.

Later, in editing, the sequence is cut together exactly in the same way as any other direct-recording sequence. When that is done, the sequence is cut into individual loops, each loop of synchronized picture and track consisting of perhaps only a sentence or two of dialogue. Then the loops are taken to a recording studio where each loop can be run continuously on the screen and the dialogue heard and the picture seen over and over. The actors listen and watch and try to repeat the sentences exactly as they did in the original shooting, to sync their voices with the lip movements in the picture. Then, with each loop, their dialogue is recorded in the almost perfect conditions of the recording room. After all loops have been recorded, the editor matches the new track with the mouth movements in the original picture sequence. Later, necessary sound effects are added, and the film appears on the screen as if it were actually direct recording.

Lip syncing makes it possible to use locations which would otherwise be out of the question. Many expensive sets are eliminated and the cost of the film cut considerably.

Lip syncing is also used in translating films from one language into another; indeed, the results of this work are often amazing.

From the director's standpoint, the lip sync process presents difficulties which make its use undesirable except as a last resort. The continual repetition of the same lines by even the best actors produces a more or less mechanical performance which completely lacks spontaneity. However, even this is more desirable than the overprojection which results when actors are forced to speak too loudly during direct recording, and the director usually chooses this alternative when noises force the mixer to ask for more volume than the actor can deliver naturally.

THE PLAY-BACK

The reverse of the lip sync process is prescoring—often referred to as the *play-back*. It is used when we wish to record the sound before shooting the picture.

Most often used in musicals, the use of the play-back requires that the music and dialogue be recorded first. Later, during the shooting, the original sound is played back over a loudspeaker on the set. The actors sing or play their instruments in sync with the play-back and concentrate on their appearance and actions. Later on in editing, the picture is synced with the original track.

In the shooting of a musical sequence, such as the playing of a number by a symphony orchestra, the production procedures used in ordinary direct recording are awkward and inappropriate. While the music is continuous, the film must cut from scene to scene. If the music were recorded synchronously with the shooting of each scene, syncing would be extremely difficult, and the music would vary slightly in volume and sound perspective at each cut. Therefore, the music is prescored and one continuous track is used for all the cuts and angles of the sequence.

Another advantage of the play-back is purely economical. Frequently, retakes are often necessary to gain a perfect recording. Furthermore, first takes are not always acceptable from a photographic and directorial standpoint. Thus, if we tried to produce good music according to the usual direct-recording procedure, the number of added takes would be doubled. That would mean added time for which the whole production crew would have to be paid. On the other hand, the cameraman, electricians, props, and grips are not needed during the prescoring, and their absence from the payroll at those times results in a substantial saving.

SOUND EFFECTS

When Alfred Hitchcock first came to the United States, he was asked, "What are you going to do now that American train whistles have a different pitch from those of English trains?" The questioner was ribbing the great English director because of his frequent use of the sound bridge dissolve. In *The Thirty-nine Steps* and also in *The Lady Vanishes,* a woman screams and the sound of the scream dissolves to the shrill whistle of a train as the picture dissolves from her face to the train. Again, in *The Girl Was Young* (*Young and Innocent*) the sound of a woman's scream dissolves to the call of sea gulls.

Hitchcock's use of the sound track to convey ideas and emotions is one of the many techniques which make him the director he is. However, such use of creative sound effects depends upon a knowledge of the mechanical principles involved.

As mentioned before, sound effects may be secured during the direct recording, and they may also be added later in the one or more effect-tracks made during editing. Footsteps, the closing and opening of doors, and the like are inherent in direct recording, but in a silent or lip-synced scene they must be added. If added, they are usually secured from the studio's sound-effects library, but in certain cases they may be recorded "wild" (without picture) for the particular purpose. Some sound which may seem inherent in a direct-recording scene must be recorded separately.

Suppose the scene is a crowded restaurant. The two principals are talking in the foreground, while life goes on in the background. The sound would be handled something like this: during the direct recording, the extras in the background make as little noise as possible. They merely mouth the movements of talking but do not make any sounds. Only the foreground dialogue is recorded. Later, a sound-effects track of the background chatter is added, and during dubbing the mixers control the balance of foreground speech which they want understood and of background sound which must be heard but not loudly enough to be confusing.

In the shooting of battle scenes, actual shells are not exploded, and blanks are often used instead of real bullets. However, the powder charges used to simulate the exploding shells have a sound entirely different from the real thing, and blanks do not sound at all like actual bullets. Thus, a separate track, with the actual sounds, is synced with the picture. In addition, a loop of miscellaneous battle sounds is usually added for the off-stage and background effects. During dubbing, this loop—or loops, as there may be several —are run continuously during the battle scenes.

The director is not expected to know, in all cases, how best to handle effects during production. Advising him is one of the duties of the mixer. Sometimes, for technical reasons, the mixer will desire to record particular effects during direct recording. At other times, he will want to subdue certain sounds and add effects later. Either way, too large a problem is seldom presented.

The director must know what effect he desires to achieve. He must understand the relationship of sound to picture and the various ways in which sound may carry an idea not conveyed by the picture. Sound effects, for the most part, are meaningless by themselves, but in association with the direct idea of the scene, or as an indirect carry-over from the story, they can convey considerable information and, at times, a tremendous emotional impact.

The scene is a close-up of a pretty little girl of ten as she plays on the steps of her suburban home. It is almost evening, and the street has previously been shown deserted. As the girl plays with her dolls, we hear the sound of approaching footsteps, irregularly spaced with that of the tapping of a cane. That, by itself, means nothing, but if previously in the film we have established that her beloved old grandfather walks with a cane, the audience will glow with happy anticipation. But what happens if we have established that a sex-crazed maniac walks with a cane? The same scene, with the same sound effect, takes on an entirely different meaning.

This simple example illustrates one of the most important principles in the use of significant sound effects. Whenever a sound effect is to be used to carry a particular meaning, it must be planted previously with the picture with which it is to be associated. Michael Curtiz had an excellent example of this in his *The Breaking Point*. Early in the film we see the mother of an impoverished family working on her sewing machine. The sound of the machine is featured. Later in the film, the husband, in bed at night, hears the same sound, and the audience immediately associates the sound with its source.

Sound effects can be used to bridge a pictorial dissolve. In Charley Turner's army documentary, *Journey to Reality*, a mental patient is introduced to the occupational rehabilitative process of sanding a board. This picture dissolves to another of the patient, in a different location, as he sands a different board. The sound of the sandpaper scratching over the wood is carried through the dissolve, but at a faster tempo, and the audience understands that during a long period of time the patient has worked steadily over the wood with his sandpaper. In addition, the interest of the audience is heightened by the peculiar audio-visual combination.

The sound bridge dissolve is often varied by having the sound effect dissolve with the picture to another sound effect having a similar pitch and quality. Such was the relation of a woman's scream to the whistle of a train, mentioned previously as having been used by Hitchcock.

As a general rule, it is desirable to approach reality as closely as possible. At times, however, sound effects are distorted in order to gain a particular emotional effect or to help the audience understand a character in the film. During the dramatic chase in the sewers of Vienna, in Carol Reed's *The Third Man*, the audience hears the distorted sounds of the posse's footsteps as its members seemingly close in on Orson Welles from every direction. In *Journey to Reality*, a music student whose emotional balance is wavering feels the noise of city traffic closing in on her. By distorting and amplifying normal effects, the film transmits her sensations to the audience. In my own *To Hear Again*, the audience hears music as "received" by hearing casualties who miss the higher and lower frequencies.

Distortion effects are usually secured by recording normally, and
then filtering the sound during the dubbing or predubbing.

Occasionally the complete lack of sound effects and music—
utter silence—can result in an emotional reaction. William Wellman's
The Next Voice You Hear is separated into seven different parts,
each part presenting the action of one day of the week. The sepa-
ration is achieved by the use of titles superimposed over a cloud
background. Usually following a sequence which builds to a climax
of sound and voice, the title scenes are shown with absolute
silence. With the dissolve to title, the sound track goes dead, and
in keeping with the theme, the audience feels a great sense of
awe and expectation. This film is interesting, too, in that there
is no background music. Only in the final scene is there the rising
crescendo of mood music.

BACKGROUND MUSIC

While the director need not be a musician, he should
have good musical taste. He should recognize appropriate themes
and know how they should be managed during dubbing. He must
know where he desires music, and he must know what type of
music he desires (i.e., mysterioso, pastoral, military, agitato, and
so on). Furthermore, he should consider the use of music at the
time he plans his other techniques, audio and visual.

Music, when a sole medium of entertainment, must stand by
itself, but motion picture background music must not, by itself,
attract attention. It must assist in guiding the mood of the audience,
but it cannot be so loud or so strong that it diverts attention from
the picture. Thus, composing good background music is an entirely
different problem from that of composing music as a self-sustaining
means of expression. Composers who excel in popular or sym-
phonic music are not necessarily gifted or trained in background
composition. Sometimes, of course, the background score of a picture will attain individual popularity, but usually, before that
happens, the piece must be altered for popular rendition. Such was

(Courtesy of RKO Radio Pictures, Inc.)

Recording the music for Howard Hawks' *The Big Sky*. Dimitri Tiomkin is conducting.

the case in *Laura*, the background music for the picture of the same name. An exception to this was *The Third Man* theme which, played on a zither, was the background music for *The Third Man*.

Generally, it is neither necessary nor desirable to have background or mood music throughout the entire film. It should be used to introduce, to guide, to punctuate. Like visual techniques and pictorial emphasis, music can be used to excess and thus fail of its purpose when really needed.

Sometimes sound effects, dialogue, and visual action should carry the story, but at other times the emphasis can be given with music, a minimum of movement, and no dialogue nor sound effects. Here, too, only good taste, imagination, and experience can be the judge.

The musical score is composed for the more expensive theatrical production, but for the less expensive short, commercial, and educational film, the "score" is merely stock music track which is assembled and cut to fit the picture. It may include track recorded for previous pictures as well as track composed and recorded as miscellaneous background music for use with any and all film made by the producing organization.

In motion picture production centers there are usually several business organizations whose sole activity is the collection of recorded sound effects and music track which they rent to producing organizations. Thus, we may hear the same piece of music in many different motion pictures.

NARRATION

Like music, narration is not written to be heard by itself, but rather to assist the picture. However, this assistance must not be obvious. Sometimes poor narration is written as a speech or expositional essay. The writer forgets that it is the picture which tells the story. Narration should merely aid or explain points which the picture cannot or does not make clear.

Good narration is unobtrusive and often like a train of thought which guides the audience as they view the film. It should seldom, if ever, sound like the prepared speech of a radio commentator. For example, the speechmaker might say, "The first step upon entering the hospital is a physical examination." Let us see what might happen if the same thought is imparted by a combination of narration and picture. The picture shows a hospital corridor. A new patient enters a door marked "Physical Examination." The narrator says, "The first step." He says no more, no less, just that phrase, and the audience understands without having their intelligence insulted by a double explanation, one in narration, one in picture.

Just as the written style of narration should be unobtrusive, so should the style of the narrator not attempt to carry the complete burden. The radio commentator and elocutionist must speak in complete sentences with a punchy, individualistic style born of the knowledge that their voices and words must carry the entire message. The film narrator, however, realizes that he must not compete with the picture, that he must not distract attention from the visual. His narration must be in complete harmony with what the audience sees.

This unobtrusive underwriting and underplaying is the key to writing and delivering narration for the pictorial continuity film. On the other hand, for the newsreel-type film, the narration must assume more of a burden and approach nearer to the radio style. The weaker the visual continuity, the stronger must be the narration. *The March of Time*, certain documentaries, and the various newsreels must depend upon the narration to carry the thought. The picture is merely illustrative. Therefore, producers of the newsreel-type film insist upon the use of a strong, punchy, narrative voice and a writing style which more closely approaches traditional exposition. On the other hand, continuity-type films, with a strong visual story line, often have narration which, by itself, might seem sketchy and incomplete.

Narrators must be cast in much the same manner as actors. I believe that in continuity-type films, radio announcers often make rather poor narrators. Trained to punch key words in traditional radio style, they carry an audio unbalance to the film that detracts from its over-all effectiveness. Much better is the actor with an appealing voice who can submerge his style in the film and still carry a feeling of sincerity. Sometimes he will even take on a particular characterization which blends with the theme. In that great army documentary, *Let There Be Light*, the voice of the late Walter Huston assumed the kindly gruffness of an old and wise doctor. The compassion and simplicity of his style lent the film a dignity in accord with its theme—the often successful treatment of battle psychosis and psychiatric patients. Likewise in the Academy Award documentary winner, *Seeds of Destiny*, Ralph Bellamy's voice blended with the picture but still had an appeal and personality of its own.

(*Courtesy of Reeves Sound Studios, Inc.*)

The dubbing or re-recording session constitutes perhaps the most important few hours in the birth of a motion picture.

The general thought line of the narration is in the original scenario, but usually it is only after the film has been shot and edited that the exact narration can be written. Narration must be cued exactly and precisely to the picture, otherwise the audience may hear one idea while their eye sees another. An idea may be verbally expressed in many different ways, and it is comparatively easy to alter words to fit the film. The film, however, cannot be so easily altered. The tempo of actions, once photographed, cannot be changed, and trying to edit continuity film to fit prewritten narration often results in a splotchy, ineffectual visual presentation. Therefore, after the film has been edited to suit the action, the narration should be rewritten from the original scenario to fit the film. This narration is recorded on the track and given to the editor for exact syncing. The editor will then do a certain amount of tightening and readjusting of the picture to make the job one.

DUBBING

Technically conducted by members of the sound department or a private, commercial sound organization, and artistically guided by the producer-director-editor-writer team, the dubbing session is perhaps the most important few hours in the birth of a motion picture.

It is in the dubbing, or re-recording as it is sometimes called, that the sounds of the entire audio—dialogue, narration, music, sound effects—are blended into one sound track. Mechanically, the process is comparatively simple. All the tracks are interlocked and run at the same time the picture is shown on the screen. The volume from each track is controlled by one of several mixers on the sound console. From a cue-sheet prepared by the editor and sound editors, the mixers know at what footages to expect certain sounds, and they are able to control the volume of the various tracks and attain the desired over-all blend. This over-all blend of sounds is recorded on one track, and dubbing is complete.

Of course, many rehearsals are needed by the mixers in order to secure the exact results desired, and frequently it is necessary to make several takes on each reel before a satisfactory result is achieved. It is not too uncommon to spend an entire day in dubbing a single reel.

In addition to blending all the various tracks into one, the dubbing session often includes the execution of many special sound effects. Filtering of voices required for telephone effects is frequently done during dubbing. Another example is the securing of an echo effect. This can be accomplished through the use of a mechanical or electronic *echo box* or of duplicate tracks of a particular sound, one track laid slightly behind the other.

The use of duplicate tracks can also be used to secure a babble

DUBBING

Editor

Music

Sound effects

Music may be recorded on track specifically for the film or it may be stock music track cut to fit.

The editor usually submits the cut picture and one or two direct recording tracks – plus any narration track.

The dubbing session

The finished film

The effects editor may submit any number of effect tracks and effect loops.

Loops merely repeat the same sounds and are brought in and out as needed by the technicians conducting the dubbing.

of many voices when only a few have been recorded. Suppose a mob scene requires a hundred shouting voices. Only twenty have previously been recorded. The sound of these twenty voices is printed on five identical tracks, and during dubbing, these five tracks are run out of sync. The result is five times twenty or one hundred voices.

Since the final dubbing session is so important to the finished film, I think it is desirable that the writer, editor, director, and the producer attend it. Each of these men has contributed ideas and life to the over-all sound effects, and only if they are present can they be sure of the end result. Too, their combined ideas often result in desirable changes which may improve the film considerably.

It must be remembered that the sound technicians conduct the dubbing according to certain principles which are applicable 95 per cent of the time. They will also apply these same principles the other 5 per cent if not prevented from doing so. For example, in one film which I directed, a battle sequence ran for almost an entire reel. Much of the battle was filmed in direct recording which contained the shouts, commands, and excited voices characteristic of men in battle. The explosions of shells and the chatter of machine guns and rifles were added in various sound-effect tracks. Now, the sound technician is trained to make sure that all dialogue is audible and understandable. In this situation, however, the explosions of battle often interfered with the audibility of much of the dialogue of the excited soldiers. The natural instinct of the sound technician was to reduce the volume of sound effects so that the dialogue might be understood, but from our point of view the dialogue was not important in itself. We wanted an effect of confused voices, shouting, and explosions, and we had to point that out to the technician conducting the dubbing.

THE CREATION OF SOUND

Much of the narration, sound effects, and musical approach is conceived by the writer and executed by the various artists and technicians. The conception of sound bridges and transitions, the mood of narration, and the desirability of music are at least implied in the scenario. It is true that the director must understand the processes involved and appreciate the effects for which he is striving; it is also true that he may add touches of his own. But the original plan is up to the writer.

The writer should have as great a consciousness of sound as the director, but once his plan is on paper, it is up to the director and his team to carry it through.

In sound, as well as in many of the other techniques and media involved in making a film, continual liaison between the writer and the director throughout the entire production will produce a much finer result on the screen.

CHAPTER EIGHT

ABOUT PRODUCTION

The making of a film is divided into three stages: writing, shooting, and editing. They may be likened to the stages of any commercial production enterprise—the building of automobiles, radios, or air conditioners. The writing stage is on a par with the drawing of the blueprint, the laying out of the plans. The shooting stage, sometimes called production, is equivalent to the manufacturing, the construction of all the essential parts. The editing stage is similar to the assembly of the parts into the completed product. While the director is sometimes in charge only of shooting, and may or may not act as a consultant or supervisor during writing and editing, he must be thoroughly familiar with all three stages. Indeed, the majority of screen directors are former editors or writers who have organizational and executive ability.

THE WRITING STAGE

The average screen director is almost entirely dependent upon the work of the scenario writer! It is the writer who designs the product, and as his work is good or bad, so is the finished film good or bad. Depending upon the tolerances allowed by the particular producing organization, the director is limited by the worth of his scenario. It is true that he may improve the dialogue and add to the camera technique or bits of actor's business, but the plan for the film is not his; it is the writer's. While a good plan can become a bad film if poorly directed, it is seldom that a poor plan becomes a good picture, even if superbly directed. Before any director can hope to make a presentable film, he must have a presentable scenario. What the film says comes from the writer, and it is he, not the director, who is basically the most important link in the producing chain.

The influence of the director upon the scenario to be filmed varies with the situation. Sometimes, particularly in the case of educational, commercial, and B entertainment films, the director has no influence. He is simply called in by the producer, presented with a completed script, and told to direct the shooting. He may or may not have the authority to make minor changes and alterations during production. However, if he is allowed no latitude, the result is almost certain to lack pictorial coherence. Very few, if any, writers are able to sit behind their typewriters in their lonely rooms and visualize and understand all the production problems which will influence the completed film. Even though the basic plan is good, if the director is allowed no latitude during production, there are certain to be rough and incongruous spots in the completed picture, places where the preproduction visualization was not complete and where the director was not allowed to use his knowledge and experience.

In many cases, the director is called in while the scenario is still in somewhat rough form. He reads the draft and then discusses it with the producer and writer. In such a situation the director has the opportunity to place his production experience and peculiar abilities at the disposal of the writer and producer with favorable effects on the cost and worth of the finished product. Under such a working arrangement, the writer is usually available to the director during preproduction planning, and changes are considered more of a sign of progress and improvement than a criminal deviation from the sacred scenario.

Sometimes it happens that the director is part of the inception of the scenario idea. The famous Brackett and Wilder team is one example of this arrangement. Sometimes the director may function in two capacities, as a writer-director or as a producer-director. Often, too, he may act in neither of these dual capacities, but has enough prestige to be called in early in the writing stage. Naturally, any of these situations is most desirable from the director's viewpoint.

The one-man picture idea can, however, be carried to an extreme. I believe that while a few geniuses may be capable of writing, producing, and directing their own films, most individuals are weak in at least one or more phases. In writing, for example, some individuals are excellent in construction, fair in visualizing pictorial continuity, and extremely weak in writing spoken dialogue. Others write excellent dialogue but are poor in original construction. Such individual differences account for the many writing credits we see on most theatrical films. Furthermore, in disagreement, argument, and the meeting of minds, there frequently emerge ideas, stories, and characters which would otherwise remain unborn.

PRE-PRODUCTION PLANNING

In one way or the other the director has been given the scenario. After a preliminary reading or two, if he was not in on the inception, he discusses it with the writer and the producer. He tries to probe the minds of both the writer and the producer and comprehend their attitudes toward the plot, characters, and possible messages. Many obscure points assume important proportions after discussion and argument. The director discovers, too, how much he is allowed to spend on the film, what the tentative shooting schedule is, the starting date, which sequences have been tentatively planned for location shooting and which sequences for studio production. He also discovers whether the producer is committed to any particular actors or has any particular desires in that regard.

After this preliminary discussion, the director probably studies the scenario again. He may make some written or mental notes. Perhaps one short sequence can be eliminated, and the money which would have been spent for it added to the account of a longer, more important sequence. Perhaps the director is unhappy with the dialogue in another sequence, or it may be that he feels the ending should have a slightly different twist.

He analyzes the sets required. Can he use any sets already constructed and standing on the stage from a previous picture? Is there any chance of so constructing the sets to be built that they can be used for two or more sets by merely changing the props and re-dressing?

After getting a thorough mental picture of the scenario and its production requirements, he resumes his discussions with the producer and writer. The director finds that some of his ideas are readily accepted, while others are quickly rejected because of factors previously unknown to him. Still other ideas of his, after discussion, are developed along completely new lines. Perhaps after some spirited argument, there is a meeting of minds, and finally, all are agreed upon the scenario and methods of production. The director is ready to go to work on the final pre-production preparations.

He coordinates the three major jobs which must be completed before the cameras roll: casting, sets and locations, and his editorial and shooting plan.

SETS AND LOCATIONS

In the large west coast studios, the search for and selection of location sites is the full-time job of a department specifically set up for that purpose. In the smaller studios and on the east coast, the job generally falls to the director.

Naturally the location site must fit the dramatic requirements of the scenario. However, there are other requirements which can complicate the selection.

The weather record of the proposed location for the past ten years is reviewed. Normally, shooting is done only in brilliant sunlight, and a few weeks of solid overcast or rain can play havoc with the budget. Other factors are the direction of the sunlight and the distance to be traveled to and from the location. Control of spectators who somehow always assemble around a motion picture crew may necessitate police protection. Passing trains, automobiles, or airplanes may make direct recording impossible.

Before a location is definitely selected, it should be surveyed by both the cameraman and the sound man. The writer, the producer, and the director may have grand ideas, but it is the technicians who actually put the picture and sound on film. They, too, have their problems.

Shortly after the director's initial conferences with the producer and the writer, he should talk to the art director. Between them they decide the general layout of each set, its size, and its character treatment.

Most art directors prefer that the director have something specific in mind for this first discussion. Thus, it is well if the director formulates some ideas during his first readings of the script and his conferences with the producer and writer.

In set design, as in composition, formal balance and regularity should be avoided. Certainly the traditional interior L set is elementary to design and easy to construct, but if all the sets in the film are of that nature, the scenes may be monotonously alike and lack the compositional movement that comes with foreground pieces, winding stairs, interesting fireplaces, and large, bay windows. However, extremes in that direction are to be avoided.

It is easy to become entranced with the camera compositional possibilities of an intricate set and to forget the basic realities of the story. That, in effect, is one of the legitimate criticisms that have been leveled against Hollywood. How often do we see the fifty-dollar-a-week clerk living in a house or apartment that is more in keeping with the fifteen-thousand-dollar-a-year executive? The director must not be overcome by artistic impulses and forget economic realities—either those of his story or of his producer!

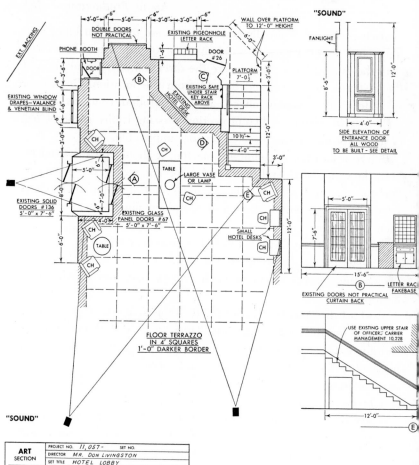

"SOUND"

FANLIGHT

12'-0"

8'-6"

4'-0"

SIDE ELEVATION OF
ENTRANCE DOOR
ALL WOOD
TO BE BUILT - SEE DETAIL

5'-0"

7'-6"

15'-6"

B

LETTER RACK
FAKEBASE

EXISTING DOORS NOT PRACTICAL
CURTAIN BACK

USE EXISTING UPPER STAIR
OF OFFICERS' CARRIER
MANAGEMENT 10,228

12'-0"

E

ART SECTION	PROJECT NO. 11,057 - SET NO.
	DIRECTOR MR. DON LIVINGSTON
STUDIO. BRANCH	SET TITLE HOTEL LOBBY
	PROJECT TITLE FACE TO FACE WITH COMMUNISM
SIGNAL CORPS PHOTOGRAPHIC CENTER	ART DIRECTOR MR. MURPHY
	SCALE 1/4" = 1'-0" DRAWN BY F. NAMCZY
	DATE DEC. 20-50
	APPROVAL 9.B.L

INT. HOTEL LOBBY
SCENES – NO. 11 THRU 23 – 72 – 73

A set plan. Most of the larger studios carry many standard items in stock, and these items are used over and over again for different sets. Here, the use of "existing" doors, stairs, hotel desk, letter rack, and safe reduce construction costs.

132

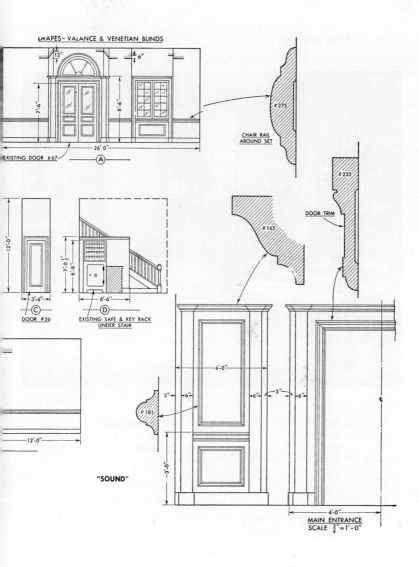

DRAPES - VALANCE & VENETIAN BLINDS

12"   6"

7'-6"   8'-6"

EXISTING DOOR #67   26'0"

A

#275

CHAIR RAIL
AROUND SET

#235

DOOR TRIM

#165

12'-0"

7'-0½"   6'-8"

3'-6"   6'-6"

C   D

DOOR #26   EXISTING SAFE & KEY RACK
            UNDER STAIR

12'-0"

4'-0"

3" 6"   #181   6" 3" 6"

3'-0"

"SOUND"

MAIN ENTRANCE
SCALE ¾" = 1'-0"

4'-0"

133

(U.S. Army Photo)

A shot on the set built from the plans on the preceding pages. Note how the stock items dress up the otherwise simple, economical construction. The unbalanced composition of this shot was corrected during the scene by a bellhop entering the lower right-hand corner of the frame.

The story and its mood, the editorial pattern and movement, the effects the director desires to secure—all must be considered in the design of the sets. In addition, the director must consider the conditions under which he will be working, the available stage space, and the budget. All these factors, of course, are part of the art director's job. However, if the director, as the over-all guiding hand, considers them, he will make the work that much easier for the art director, and in the end, for himself.

For example: it is expected that there will be considerable low-level dialogue in one of the sets. That set should be placed in the quietest of the sound stages, and the floors and walls of the set should be acoustically treated. Such precautions may avoid an unfortunate director-sound man controversy during production.

The director should remember the problems of his cameraman, too. Indeed, before approving any set for construction, he should have his cameraman study the plans. There must be clearance for the lights, room for the camera, and working space for the crew.

The art director, too, may broach many more questions, for set design is his job. The director must respect his training and ability.

After the director and the art director agree on all aspects of a set, the designers go to work on the plans. Later, when the plans are completed, the director may be asked to sign them, for last-minute changes can sometimes throw the carpenters into a dither.

As the sets begin to assume their proportions on the stage, the director may be called in from time to time to answer questions about items not too clear in the plans and of which the art director is uncertain. Perhaps the carpenters and painters will want to know how close the camera will come to a particular door. Problems may arise as to whether the paneling should be constructed in bold relief or merely painted. Sometimes the director himself may ask for minor alterations. At one point, he may discover that he will be shooting off the set, and he may ask for an additional four-foot wing.

Simultaneously with the design and building of the sets and the search for locations, the director casts and makes his editorial and movement plans. Too, his crew is probably being hired or assigned, and he is discussing plans and production problems with his key men.

THE CREW

The number and types of specialists on a production crew vary with the size and nature of the scenes to be shot. On minor locations, only a cameraman and an assistant may be assigned to the camera. Larger locations and studio work may require a director of photography who is in charge of the camera crew, an operating cameraman who pans, tilts, and otherwise operates the camera, and one or more assistant cameramen. The assistants load the magazines and change the film, make "slop" tests of exposed film, keep necessary records of scenes, takes, and footages exposed, change lenses, operate the clapsticks, and slate the scenes. On particularly large sets, such as battle or mob scenes, where several cameras are used, there are usually an operating cameraman and one or more assistants for each camera.

The sound crew usually consists of the standard organization mentioned previously: a mixer, a recordist, and a boom man. On large, exterior sets, additional sound men may be needed.

The production crew may, or may not, include the following: One or more assistant directors, a unit manager, a script clerk, any number of juicers depending on the lights which must be manned, any number of grips depending on the amount of manual labor expected, several property men, powder men, and make-up men.

Handling this crew, this complex group of skills, is primarily the job of the assistant director. But the assistant works under the director, and to the director falls the responsibility for the morale and efficiency of the group.

Just as a general is helpless without his troops, so is a director helpless without his crew. No one man can make a picture. Thus, the director must be as well versed in the art of leadership as in the art of the film. Frequently, worthy ideas originate from the props, grips, and electricians, and the director who is too proud to make use of them is overlooking a wealth of material. The director who makes each member of the crew an interested and happy member of the team is well on the road to a good picture.

THE ASSISTANT DIRECTOR

The assistant director handles the administrative and organizational details of production. His mission is to free the hands of the director so that the latter may concentrate on the story and

DAILY PRODUCTION CALL SHEET

PROJECT NO. 22089	TITLE	THE MILITARY FUNERAL	DATE 27 May 1952
PROJECT OFFICER Mr. Ed. Warren	DIRECTOR Mr. Don Livingston		ASSISTANT DIRECTOR Mr. Richard Allen

SET OR LOCATION	CAST	WARDROBE
INTERIOR: Anderson Living Room Stage E Staff and Crew 0830	Mrs. Anderson: Jeanne Shepherd Chaplain Gilbert: George Kluge Lt. Grady: Charles Nolte CALL: 0830	Simple house dress Class "A" Uniform with Ike Jacket (OD'S) SOUND WILL WORK

LUNCH CALL

DISTRIBUTION:

Studio Division
Proj. Off. Branch
Casting Section
Studio Props
Make up
Camera Branch
Sound
File

ADVANCE SHOOTING NOTES

DATE	SET OR LOCATION	SCENE NUMBERS
28 May 1952	Same as above	50 thru 66

SIGNATURE OF ASSISTANT DIRECTOR   Richard Allen

An example of a Daily Production Call Sheet. In the larger studios, the assistant director for each crew or "company" prepares a similar form designed to keep the various departments informed concerning the crew's activities.

its presentation. It is the assistant, and sometimes the unit manager, who prepares the production breakdown,* the shooting schedule,† and the call sheets which list the place, time, and names of the crew and actors who are to report each day.

On the set, the assistant handles the crew and expedites the production. He maintains order, calls for quiet during sound takes, and directs background action according to the plan of the director.

On larger sets, there may be one or more second assistant directors—*herders*, as they are sometimes called—whose primary job is to handle the many extras.

THE UNIT MANAGER

The unit manager is the financial representative of the front office. He maintains a constant check on the expenditure of funds and keeps the director informed if the budget is being exceeded. The unit manager also makes necessary arrangements with commercial and governmental organizations and private individuals for the use of location areas, hotel lodging of crew and actors, and the lease of automobiles and other large items.

The division of function between the unit manager and assistant director varies somewhat from studio to studio.

THE SCRIPT CLERK

The script clerk acts as the director's memory. He—or she, for this employee frequently is a girl—keeps constant notes on every take of every scene. She notes the positions and dialogue of actors so that actions can be matched in scenes to be shot later, and she writes a description of each scene to assist the editor in cutting the film.

* See definition of breakdown, p. 168.
† See definition of schedule, p. 168.

Shooting exteriors on location for *The Big Sky*, directed by Howard Hawks. The grips have erected a high parallel on which the camera is being mounted.

THE JUICERS

The juicers are the electricians who handle the lights for the cameraman or director of photography. The chief juicer or boss electrician is called the *gaffer*, and his assistant the *best boy*.

Frequently the gaffer does the preliminary blocking in of the lights, and the director of photography puts in the finishing touches later.

THE GRIPS

Motion picture production requires a very specialized type of manual labor. The men who perform this are called *grips*.

Shooting exteriors in the studio for Warner Brothers' *Night and Day,* directed by Michael Curtiz. The old standby substitute for falling snow is cream of maize, a special type of cornflakes. Various chemical solutions are also used for fallen snow, known as "dress snow."

The grips must lay the tracks for the dolly and push it at the exact speed required for the scene. They mount the camera on the tripod or dolly and move it where needed for each scene. When the camera must be mounted high in the air, they build the parallels or large platforms for it. They move wild walls of the set, provide necessary rigging, and do the many other manual jobs incident to production.

THE PROP MEN

The prop men (property men) secure and become responsible for the items and equipment to be photographed. The pack of cigarettes in the leading man's pocket, the letter to be mailed, the pen used to sign the check, the check itself, the pistol used by the heavy, the stethoscope used by the doctor—all these things are obtained and cared for by the prop men. In addition, they keep track of the dressing of the set so that it may match from scene to scene.

On the east coast, the prop men handle all properties on the set, but on the west coast, the work is broken down into different categories. *Greens men* handle the foliage and trees on the set, and *set dressers* handle furniture and the pictures on the walls.

One of the industry's favorite stories concerns a certain famous director and his prop man. They had worked together for years, and regardless of what the director asked for, the prop man always had it available. It was the prop man's boast that he had never been stumped!

One time, on location in the middle of the Arizona Desert, the director decided to put an end to his helper's bragging. There, miles from civilization and vegetation, the director asked for a fresh—a fragrantly fresh—red rose. The prop man had it in exactly fifteen minutes!

That director is still muttering to himself.

THE MAKE-UP MEN

Perhaps more publicized than others in the crew, the make-up man must work in conjunction with the cameraman, for make-up and its application depend a great deal upon the cameraman's lighting.

When the lights are balanced for the varying grays of the walls and the costumes of the actors, white skin tones have a tendency to *wash out*. It is just another example of the fact that film does not have the latitude of the human eye. Thus, most cameramen desire that the actors be made up with the darkening tones of panchromatic make-up. Varying from dark yellow to brown, actors in their make-up often appear as if they were suffering from a severe attack of yellow jaundice. But, to the color-blind, black-and-white film they have the smooth skin tones the human eye finds so pleasing. Not only is the light flesh balanced to the darker surrounding tones, but skin blemishes and facial lines are less perceptible. Color photography make-up offers additional problems.

Obtaining special make-up effects also falls to the lot of the make-up men. These may include aging, scars, burns—and who can forget Frankenstein's monster and *The Hunchback of Notre Dame*?

The documentary trend just after World War II has had a continuing influence on make-up. In order to secure a more realistic newsreel effect, some directors and producers insist that actors perform without make-up. I am somewhat sympathetic toward this trend, particularly in the case of male performers. For too long now, theatrical films have pictured people as being one of two extremes—either completely ugly or completely handsome. Some leading men appear to have a complexion more suitable to the leading lady. Character lines, which often document a man's strength of character, have been eliminated in the interests of glamorization. It is time that we begin to realize that the American public has grown up and is no longer so interested in "escape" literature and films.

PRODUCTION CONFERENCES

Some time before shooting begins, there may be a formal production conference. It may be attended by the producer, the director, the cameraman, the sound man, the art director, the gaffer, the senior grip, the prop man, and various studio executives.

Usually such a meeting is little more than a formality and serves only to tie up loose ends and as a source of information to studio executives. The director already will have had many discussions with his producer and crew members. He and the producer, prior to the conference, have settled on the treatment, the schedule, the sets, the locations, and the cast. The director has outlined the mood of the film, the sets, and the types of movement and composition to the cameraman. He has briefed the sound man on any particular problems which may concern the latter, and the art director has already begun working on the set plans. The director has given the grips an idea of any unusual rigging which may be needed, and he has discussed wardrobe, special props, and explosions with the particular individuals concerned. With the leads and supporting players he has discussed the story and perhaps even held some pre-production rehearsals. He has reviewed the schedule with the assistant director, suggesting changes which he feels may expedite production or improve the film.

Thus, a formal production conference may be little more than a rehash of known problems. However, this does not mean it is a waste of time. If properly conducted, it can help straighten out conflicting interests of different technicians and help weld the group into a smooth, well-organized team.

PRE-PRODUCTION REHEARSALS

In the past few years, some directors have taken advantage of what might be called pre-production rehearsals. Usually, during production, considerable time is consumed while the actors rehearse. It is impracticable to do much lighting or camera-rehearsing until the action is pretty well jelled, and this is time wasted for the crew. Thus, preproduction rehearsals for the cast accomplish a twofold purpose: they eliminate wasted time for the crew, and they enable the actors to give a more finished performance.

The disadvantages of such a procedure depend primarily on the salaries of the actors and the contracts under which they are employed. If the actors are so highly paid that the extra days of rehearsing amount to more than the time lost on the set in terms of dollars, then, obviously, preproduction rehearsals are not economically sound. However, the advantages in better performances cannot be questioned—except by those few who decry the possible lack of spontaneity. I have found that the good professional actor grows better with repeated rehearsals.

The worth of pre-production rehearsals usually depends upon the actors' salaries, their contract arrangements, their capabilities, and the budget for the picture.

SHOOTING

The public's conception of a motion picture crew at work is usually that of a confusing galaxy of lights, cameras, microphones, sets, "emoting" actors and languid actresses, scurrying stagehands, concentrating technicians, and shouting assistants revolving about a comfortable canvas chair. In that chair, on the back of which is printed the great man's name, sits the director, calmly drinking a Coca Cola, giving orders, and stirring not a muscle of his own.

The conception of a spectator who one day gets the opportunity to observe studio production might be entirely different.

For what seems like hours, he watches members of the crew stand about and chat with one another. Finally, one of them calls to the director, who is casually talking to one of the actors.

"We're ready."

"Okay," answers the director. "Let's try a rehearsal, and then we'll make it."

There is a burst of activity as a heretofore obscure individual suddenly becomes very important. He yells, "Okay, now. Let's get it quiet for a rehearsal. Don't want to put the bells on unless I have to. Quiet, now! Quiet!"

After the rehearsal, which covers only a few lines of dialogue, the director talks a little to the actors. Then he snaps loudly to no one in particular, "All right, let's make it."

There is another burst of activity as the vociferous one again yells for everybody to be quiet. Nobody seems to pay any attention until the loud one yells, "Bells, Gus."

After the loud clanging of the warning bell, the set becomes quiet, and another heretofore obscure individual steps in front of the camera with a board on which are printed a lot of numbers and

The director guides and coordinates all the various activities on the set in such a way that the individual scenes filmed there will cut together to tell the desired story. On one of the author's sets, many of these activities are laid out in panorama.

some names. At the same time, another man calls, "Justa minute." He rushes out on the set and proceeds to pat an actor's face with Kleenex.

"Roll 'em."

"Rolling."

"Speed."

The words come from remote parts of the set, and the observer doesn't see who is calling them.

Suddenly, the man with the board in front of the camera calls out, "Project two-four-six-one, Scene twenty, Take one." He slaps a hinged stick to the board, steps away from in front of the camera, and loses himself in the group around the camera.

The observer can't see the director now; the latter, too, has lost himself in the group around the camera. But his voice calls out, "Action."

The actors start through the scene, say about two lines, when the director interrupts, "Cut it, cut it."

Noise and confusion, the clang of a bell, and the whole process is repeated.

Finally, after two or three more failures, the action runs as far as did the rehearsals. The director says, "Cut it. Okay for me." Then he talks quietly for a moment to the chap who had originally told him they were ready.

Everybody stands about and talks as the director and several of the actors wander off for cokes.

Bizarre as it may seem, the casual observer's impression is rather typical. To the inexperienced eye, film production seems a slow, inefficient, time-consuming procedure. The experienced eye judges production, not by apparent industry or the lack of it, but by the number of shooting days required to photograph a given film, the economy of cost variables, and the worth of the finished film. Had our observer been more experienced, he would have known that the two men holding a conversation by the camera were the director of photography and his gaffer. The cameraman was telling his gaffer what lighting effects he wanted. The gaffer, in turn, was telling the juicers what lights to use, which way to turn them, how to gobo them, and how many scrims to use. The operating cameraman and the two grips, behind the camera, were discussing the short dolly-in, while near-by the director was giving the actors some last-minute instructions.

When he had finished lighting the set, the cameraman so informed the director. The assistant director quieted the set informally so that carpenters, working on another set on the same stage, would not be disturbed by the bells, the official command for silence. The "character" with the Kleenex was a make-up man who noted a few beads of perspiration on the forehead of the lead.

At the start of the take, the assistant director's call, "Roll 'em," was the signal for both sound and camera. "Rolling" was the answer of both, and "Speed" was the signal to cue the slate boy that the recorder was up to speed.

After the scene was completed, the director advised the cameraman, "You won't have to move the camera for the next one. It's Scene fifty-six. The movement is exactly the same, but it should be a low-key effect. Same composition. How long will it take you?"

"About fifteen minutes," answered the cameraman. "But don't you have any more daylight effects on this set? It's easier to move the camera now than to try to match my lighting later."

"Nope. That was the last one. We can wrap it up here after three night shots. Okay?"

"Okay."

"I'll be back in ten or fifteen minutes." The director left the set to go over the next scene with his actors without interfering with the work of the cameraman.

LINING UP THE SHOT

The seemingly simple procedure of explaining to the cameraman the composition and movement desired can sometimes be perplexing to the director. If that which we see were easy to describe, there would be little reason for pictures and far less conflicting testimony in our courts. Words have many shades of meanings, and the mental vision of the speaker is often quite different from the vision he creates in the mind of the listener. Merely describing the scene desired is not always the best way to transfer the idea from director to cameraman.

When the scene is a simple close-up of an actor, most directors simply tell the cameraman, "A close-up cutting about here and from this angle." The director indicates the point at the neck or chest at which he desires the bottom frame line and he points out the camera axis.

If the scene is a static two or three shot most directors follow much the same procedure. They point out the side lines and the angle of the camera. However, when camera or subject movement is involved, or when a particular effect is desired, the director must be a diplomat as well as an artist.

While most directors understand the basic principles of camera and lenses, very few understand more than mere basic principles. Furthermore, the director has enough to do to handle his own problems without dictating technical decisions which are rightfully the concern of the cameraman. The cameraman has made the study of lenses and composition a great part of his life's work, and the overly eager director who dictates too strongly is apt to lose much of the worth of his cameraman's experience, and, too, make that individual somewhat resentful.

The director must convey to the cameraman what he wants to see on the screen without dictating the exact spot for the camera or the lens to be used.

One method of accomplishing this is the use of the same method as described for the simple close-up—indicating the angle and frame limits at each position and movement and, if it is important to the scene, the frame lines for both foreground and background. While this procedure does give the cameraman the utmost freedom and opportunity, it is time-consuming, frequently leads to misconceptions, and limits, to a certain extent, the visual thinking of the director himself.

Another method involves the use of the view-finder which can be detached from the studio camera. The actors walk through their scene, and the director views the action through the finder. The director then has the actors repeat their actions, and the cameraman views the scene through the finder from the same position or positions from which the director viewed it. The director tells the cameraman that is what he wants, but he makes it clear that

the particular lens which happens to be on the finder is not necessarily the one to be used. That decision is up to the cameraman.
The advantage of this procedure is that it gives the cameraman a
definite visual picture of what is wanted without limiting his re-
sourcefulness. Too, it gives the director an opportunity to view his
approximate composition and movement and to make corrections
before the cameraman goes to work.

Whatever the procedure, it must transmit all the director's ideas
with unmistakable clarity to the cameraman without restricting the
cameraman's creative freedom. Primarily it is a problem in leadership and teamwork.

TECHNICAL PERFECTION VERSUS ARTISTIC PERFECTION

All too often film-makers and their technicians judge
films by their own standards rather than the standards of the future
audiences. We who make pictures are constantly aware that the
film is only "play-acting," and we therefore forget the importance
of maintaining the illusion of reality. Rather, we stress technical
standards about which our audience is not even aware.

How often do we hear the studio visitor say, "It's all a fake. I'll
never enjoy another picture."

Of course, the visitor does not really mean that he thought the
actors were real cowboys, policemen, or gangsters. He is merely
expressing his admiration for the film-maker's art, which in the
past caused him to believe, for the time, what he saw on the screen.
When he first sees the flimsy sets, the horde of technicians, and the
vast outlay of technical equipment, he is shocked into the vivid
realization that the film is but a photographed play upon a lifelike
stage.

That realization, which is so shocking to the visitor, has long been
a part of the film-maker. Being unable to forget that the film is an
illusion, the motion picture technician does not live with the action
as does the average audience for which the film was made. Rather,

the cameraman watches the photography, the composition, and the lighting. The sound man is interested in the technical perfection of the sound, and the art director in the design of the sets.

Mr. Average Audience is not even aware of these aspects; in a subconscious way they influence his reaction to the film, but his conscious reaction is concerned only with the story and the action. Technical imperfections which may annoy a cameraman or a sound man go unnoticed. If carried to extremes, bad lighting, unbalanced composition, or poor sound will, of course, break the illusion, but minor imperfections will not.

Since implausible situations or unconvincing actions are first noticed by the audience, we who make films must let nothing mar the story or the reality of the actions. They must be as authentic as we can make them, and if photography, sound, or set design must suffer in so doing, this is unfortunate but preferable to destruction of the illusion we have striven so hard to create.

MEETING THE SCHEDULE

The production of motion pictures is a business, and like any other business, involves adhering to strict production schedules. Meeting those schedules—shooting all the necessary scenes in the limited time allowed—is one of the major problems of the director.

The good director plans each scene well in advance and decides in what order the scenes will be shot so as to cause the least amount of lighting changes and camera moves. On any given set, he shoots all his long shots at one time, all his close-ups of a given character at another time, and so on, without regard to the continuity of the picture. While doing this, of course, he must be certain that the scenes will cut together smoothly and that the pace of the action will be constant from scene to scene.

To reduce production time, the director uses many other tricks and *cheats*. I will take up some of them in Chapter Nine, devoted exclusively to the economic aspect.

EDITORIAL NOMENCLATURE

In order to understand what happens to the film after it has been shot, it is necessary to know the meaning of various editorial terms.

Original negative is the film which is run through the camera and recorder during production. Immediately after processing or developing, the laboratory makes a print from the exposed original negative. This print constitutes the *rushes* or the *dailies* which are screened to evaluate each day's production.

The *work print* is the title given to the rushes after they are cut together by the editor. It is the film during the editorial stage, and with this the editor spends most of his time.

Fine grain is a black-and-white, fine-grain, positive print which, for any number of reasons, is printed from the original negative. From this fine grain, the laboratory can print a duplicate or *dupe negative*.

After the work print has been approved for dubbing, it is sent to a negative matching department. There, the original negative or sometimes dupe negative is matched and spliced together, scene for scene, frame for frame, with the work print.

The *negative track* secured from dubbing is printed, together with the matched picture negative, on a *fine-grain master positive*. From this fine-grain master positive are secured any number of *master dupe negatives*. From the master dupe negatives are printed the *release prints* which go out for distribution and projection.

The facilities and mechanical aids which the editor uses are unique to his trade. For example, there are several types of *Moviolas* which he uses to view the film. *Moviola* is simply a trade name given by the company which manufactures the articles, and since there are no other similar articles of a professional nature, the trade name now means an editorial viewing machine, much as the name *Kodak* was once synonymous with the amateur still camera.

The silent Moviola is an affair which features an intermittent movement giving the illusion of movement to the film, a variable speed

(Courtesy of Moviola Manufacturing Co.)

Two of the editor's most important tools.

The synchronizer which is used to keep the picture and track in sync.

The Moviola which is used to view the film and listen to the sound.

motor, and a magnifying glass to view the moving image.

The sound Moviola has, in addition, a sound-recording head for separate track, a loud-speaker or earphones, a linking device to sync sound and picture, and a constant speed motor which runs the film at ninety feet a minute, the standard projection speed.

The *director's Moviola,* seldom used, features a rear projection device to show the image on a large, frosted glass. It is useful when several people wish to view the film at one time.

Another tool of the editor is the *synchronizer,* an affair involving film sprocket wheels on a common axis. By means of the synchronizer, the editor is able to keep his picture and various tracks in sync with one another.

The *splicer* is the instrument used to glue the film together in mechanically perfect, enduring splices so that the spliced film will run smoothly through the projector. Splicing is usually done by an assistant cutter, the editor having previously cut the film and connected the pieces to be spliced by means of paper clips.

THE EDITING PHASE

Just as the director's relationships with the writer and the scenario vary, so do arrangements with respect to his influence upon the editing.

In some situations, the director has nothing to do with the film after it is shot; in other situations, he acts as an adviser or supervisor until final dubbing. In still other situations, he retains control until the screening of the rough cut, whereupon control is transferred to the producer. Since the various procedures depend almost as much upon the individual director's personality as they do upon the organizational setups of the different studios, we will make no attempt to analyze them. Rather, we will follow the mechanical steps in the development of the film from rushes to release prints. These steps must be followed, regardless of the control setup and regardless of the director-editor relationship.

During production, the previous day's rushes are viewed each morning. After the viewing, the editor takes them to his cutting room where his assistant breaks them down. Breaking down the film is the process of cutting each scene into a separate little roll by itself. These little rolls are usually marked with grease pencil as to scene and take number and then arranged in their numerical order so that they can be found easily later on.

While the film is being broken down, the assistant editor lists, for the file, the edge numbers of each scene. Edge numbers are simply consecutive numbers, one to each foot of film, placed on the edge of the negative during manufacture, and they transfer to the positive during printing. They are used for matching negatives and ordering fine grains and any required reprints.

Furthermore, in the case of live sound, the film is often coded. Coding is a process of mechanically printing additional numbers on the edge of both picture and track. The same number is printed on each so that it becomes a simple process to synchronize the track with its corresponding picture.

As soon as the editor has sufficient film to cover a sequence or two, he may begin his first cut. Usually the first cut is quite long, and no attempt is made to pace or time it. Sometimes it is merely made up of master scenes. Cut-ins will be inserted later. Later, too, the editor will shorten and rearrange scenes in order to secure tempo, timing, and dramatic effect. Up until final dubbing, the film is in a continuing state of change aimed at improvement.

It is in the editing that the worth of the director's knowledge and the accuracy of his work become evident. Did he allow sufficient overlap of action so that the editor has a choice of matched action spots in which to cut from scene to scene? Does the tempo of action from scene to scene remain constant or vary according to desired changes of pace? Does the direction of look and movement match so that scenes cut together smoothly? Has he shot sufficient cut-aways?

If the director has done a good job editorially, the editor finds that the film almost falls into place, and he can concentrate on emphasis, pace, and dramatic values. He can even add to the dramatic job done by the director.

If the director has done a poor job editorially, even a superior dramatic job may become lost. The editor must expend all his efforts in overcoming the editorial mistakes and in so doing may have to sacrifice many of the other values present.

Eventually, however, the editor will complete a *rough cut*. The film begins to take shape and the producer and the director view it with considerable interest. The pay-off is approaching. They see emerging the fruit of all their labors, and who can blame them if they are supercritical? They decide to delete this scene, add a few frames to that scene, and take off a few frames from the beginning of another scene.

The editor begins to pace and really edit his film. If there is narration, the writer, too, must contribute his talent. The narrative ideas of the scenario must be rewritten so that they cue exactly with the picture. The film is projected time and again as writer, producer, director, and editor criticize, change, and reconsider. Nothing can be sacred. The director must be prepared to see many

An editor at work. Eric Lawrence, of *The March of Time,* syncs tracks and picture.

of his pet ideas land on the cutting room floor if they do not pay off.

At some time, however, the producer will decide he has a final cut. This final cut is shown to studio executives and other interested parties for reaction and criticism. Usually, a few more changes will result, but eventually the cut is ready for any narration to be included. After narrating, the editor lays in the track secured thereby, and adjusts, tightens, and edits some more. Some more screenings, discussions, and adjustments follow. Finally, when picture and track supplement each other harmoniously, the film is ready for opticals, sound effects, and music.

Sound effects and music are each laid in their separate tracks, as discussed in the chapter on sound. While this is being done, an optical department or agency is preparing the fades, wipes, and dissolves.

Having decided on the position, number, type, and length of his opticals, the editor orders from the laboratory fine grains of all scenes on both sides of all opticals. These fine grains are turned over to the optical agency where the opticals are printed in the form of dupe negatives. The dupe negative replaces the original negative of the same scenes in the master negative of the film. Prints from the dupe negative optical scenes are used to replace the scenes of the work print, so that when the film goes into dubbing the sound technicians may be able to see the exact, final picture transitions as they mix the sound transitions.

After dubbing, as far as the director, producer, writer, editor, and production crew are concerned, production is complete. All that remains is the reaction of their picture's audiences. That is the final pay-off.

TELEVISION

In the introduction to this book, I mentioned the effect of television upon the motion picture industry. I noted that from a creative viewpoint there is little difference between the two media. Specifically, there are but three deviations in technique. In television extreme low-key lighting must be avoided, pans must be slower, and close-ups should be used more frequently. Methods of production, on the other hand, vary widely.

The production methods of the live television show are so different from motion picture production methods that the film director who would direct television must learn much. True, his knowledge of the screen technique is basic for both media and the psychology

(Courtesy of NBC

The live television show is usually produced by means of three or more cameras, and the show is played in continuity like a stage play. As the cameras are moved about for their different angles, the director in the control room selects the scenes to be telecast. All this, of course, is carefully preplanned and rehearsed. This scene is from Philco's Television Playhouse, *I Like it Here.*

of leadership remains constant, but mechanical methods alter considerably the way in which he must secure his results. Furthermore, he must realize that many of the pictorial niceties of the motion picture screen are quite impracticable on the live television show. Note the following contrasts:

In film production, each scene is secured separately. Elaborate preparations may be made for just one effect, and many trials can be made until the effect is perfect. Moreover, the actor and the cameraman can work primarily for the scene alone. Only the director need think much in terms of the total effect.

The television director sits at a console and watches the monitoring screens of the different cameras. He indicates to the technical director what cameras are to be telecast, and the technical director makes the actual changes.

In live television, the whole show is produced as a unit. Since several cameras are used, it is impossible to light for one angle only or to shoot angles which might place the camera in the field of another camera.

Mistakes in film production simply mean retakes or elimination by the editor.

Mistakes in television are sent out over the air and into millions of homes.

In film production, the director may require another take if he dislikes an actor's performance.

In television, he is almost helpless. When live television goes on the air, the director loses almost all control. The show becomes the "first night" of the theater.

Except for the use of film, the dramatic television show is limited to the studio, and the inspiring exteriors so common to the film screen are impossible.

Finally, the movie can be shown over and over again, during hours best suited to the local time zone, but the live show is televised over a network only once, with further broadcasts limited to the unsatisfactory kinescope.

For these reasons, I believe that eventually much of television's entertainment, particularly the dramatic play, will be produced on film. Methods of accomplishing this within limited television budgets are being tried with varying degrees of success. Here lies a great future.

CHAPTER NINE

THE COMMERCIAL ASPECT

The production of a motion picture costs money, usually many thousands of dollars. Therefore, when a producer invests in or secures backing for a film, he has a very definite purpose in mind. If it is to be a theatrical picture, his purpose is to bring in more money at the box office than was spent in producing it. If it is to be an advertising film, his purpose is to increase his sales profit by more than the cost of the film. If it is to be an educational film, his purpose is to train people faster and better than he could by traditional means. Yes, it may be startling news to many creative artists, but just like shoes, automobiles, and felt hats, motion pictures are produced for but one purpose—to make money!

Since the purpose is financial, it is not strange that films are paid for by business men who want them produced by business-like methods. However, producing shoes, automobiles, and felt hats require one type of production; producing motion pictures requires an entirely different type. Shoes and automobiles are produced in mass quantities, many thousands of identical items, all from the same production line. Motion pictures are produced individually, each different from the others, and many of the methods which work so efficiently in mass production are useless in film production. Furthermore, shoes or automobiles may be designed by an artist, but the actual manufacturing job is taken over by an efficient production expert, indifferent to the imagination of the creator.

But consider the problem of the film producer! He must continue to combine art and industry until the film is complete.

Understand, then, that the production of motion pictures is probably the one industry in the world which is entirely devoted to producing individual items, each different from the others, and in which the actual production is handled by a crew of many artists and technicians. It is a mixture of art and industry, imagination and fact; the man, himself an artist, who directly supervises the production is the motion picture director. His is the problem of making a film so interesting that it will draw at the box office, sell more shoes, or train better soldiers, and he must do it at a cost which will leave a margin for the original purpose—to make money.

Naturally enough, the financial end of film production is usually handled by business men who have some knowledge of production, but the director himself cannot disregard the commercial aspect. He must understand that there is a limit to his budget, he must know what constitutes the major expenditures, he must know how to get the most from the finances allotted, and sometimes he may even be expected to help in the budgeting, buying, renting, hiring, firing, and paying.

TYPES OF PRODUCING ORGANIZATIONS

The director's commercial responsibilities vary with the producing organization for which he works. In some of the larger studios, he is responsible simply for confining his sets and his cast within certain limits and for completing the shooting within a given schedule. On the other hand, he may be directing a commercial film for a small, independent organization, and he must be producer, director, unit manager, and assistant director all in one. He must personally hire, fire, and pay all the actors, crew members, and other technicians, and he must rent and pay for the stage space and studio equipment. He must draft his own schedule, make all calls and arrangements, and be personally responsible for producing the film for a given amount of money.

In order to understand why there is such a variance, let us examine the different types of producing organizations. The best known, of course, are the *majors*, the mammoth Hollywood installations which produce the majority of today's theatrical features. The majors are self-contained units which own all their own equipment and stage space and have on the regular pay roll most of the technicians and artists necessary for production. Their overhead continues, regardless of production, and the economic problem is the integrated scheduling of many productions. In such studios, the director is usually given certain limits in his schedule and sets, and his problem is merely to stay within those bounds. He is expected to concentrate on the creative end of the picture.

The *independents* are another type of producing organization. Such companies have a few key personnel on the regular pay roll, but they must hire the technicians and crews, and rent equipment and space for each individual production. In such a set-up, the director will naturally have more strict and exacting limits. His budget is often smaller, and running over the schedule causes more serious complications than in the major studio. Depending on the organization of the independent, he may or may not be expected to keep track of many financial aspects which he would not be expected to handle in the major studio.

If the director happens to be working for a minor independent— particularly if it is a one- or two-man outfit working on a shoestring —he becomes much more involved. He may be called upon to perform all the functions ordinarily allotted to the unit manager, the assistant director, and the producer.

Within these general types of companies, the director's responsibilities may vary with his prestige and personality, the type of film, the size of the budget, and the many other variables which make each film a different project all its own.

For example, in a major studio, if an art director goes overboard on several pictures, he is likely to find himself suddenly under close surveillance of studio executives. The art director then goes to the other extreme. The director, therefore, has to fight to get what he needs in the way of sets. How he conducts this fight depends upon his personality and the situation.

The unit manager may be a political power in the organization, and if the director does not get along with him socially, there are apt to be difficulties. Of course, the director may be the political power, and the unit manager a nonentity. Too, improper studio scheduling may have placed a fairly low-budget film in an over-all slack period, with the result that it gets better treatment than it deserves.

It is not the purpose of this book to cover the work of the unit manager, nor do we wish to become too involved in questions of production financing. On the other hand, the reader should realize that while in a few cases the director must become a business man, in most cases his creative instincts are tempered by the limits of the unstretchable dollar. Our purpose is to find some of the tricks he uses to get the most from what is given him. To do that, we must first examine some of the costs typical to most motion pictures.

THE "TYPICAL" BUDGET

There is no "typical" budget. Stories, sets, studios, locations, and handling vary so widely that it is impossible to call any budget typical. Furthermore, it is difficult to examine exact expenditures as related to a given picture, for, quite naturally, all studios hold that information in strict confidence.

However, we are able to show the figures of one film produced in 1947 by a major studio. It was a theatrical feature, a dramatic story and not a musical, made partly on location and partly in the studio. The stars, story, and director were all topflight. The shooting schedule was sixty-five days.

Above the line costs (costs contracted before production):

Producer and his unit	$ 70,000
Story and continuity	100,000
Director	110,000
Cast	175,000
	$455,000

Below the line costs:

Extras	$ 40,000
Set design and construction	159,000
Properties	45,000
Operating labor	60,000
Lighting	50,000
Music	50,000
Make-up	50,000
Wardrobe	15,000
Unit manager	7,000
Assistant directors	10,000
Cameraman and crew	31,000
Editing	19,000
Still photographs	6,000
Laboratory	30,000
Sound	32,000
Miscellaneous	61,300
Transportation	
Meals and lodging	
Location expense	
Titles	
Publicity	
Insurance	
Special shots	
Research	
Tests	
General overhead figured on a per-diem charge of $3,500 per day	200,000
	$1,336,000

Assuming that all personnel but the producer, the director, and the top stars worked on a wage rate rather than a job basis, we find that the following costs were in direct ratio to the time spent in actual shooting:

Salaries:

Cast (estimate one-half total figure of $175,000)	$ 87,000
Operating labor	60,000
Make-up	50,000
Unit manager	7,000
Assistant directors	10,000
Cameraman and crew	31,000

Salaries and/or rentals:

Properties	45,000
Lighting	50,000
Wardrobe	15,000
Overhead	200,000
	$555,000

The following costs bore no relationship to production time, but they were influenced by decisions of the director:

Set design and construction	$159,000
Laboratory	30,000
	$189,000

Thus, we find that the director had control over spending almost half the budget. By decisions which would lengthen or shorten the schedule, by his set requirements, and by the amount of film he used, he could materially increase or decrease half the cost of the production. The greater part of that half, however, was directly in proportion to the time spent in shooting.

Time is the most important factor as far as the director is concerned. In the foregoing example, for each day the director could have cut off his schedule, he could have saved $3,500 in overhead, plus the wages of actors, extras, and crew. In addition, he could have saved on rentals and electricity.

As mentioned previously, no budget is typical, but a study of any film budget will reveal the same answer. The most important single economic aspect is *time*. Even in the less expensive east coast commercial films, a thousand dollars a day is considered a round working figure for stage space and equipment.

Yes, time costs money, and the director must concentrate on getting the best possible picture in the least possible time.

The next most important aspect is set design and construction. The director must know how to get the most from a given set, and categorically limit his sets to a given budget.

The remainder of the budget items are relatively unimportant. However, the director must not disregard them. Film stock costs money, and the director must have a good answer if he uses too much of it. But in comparison with time, the cost of film is negligible. Thus, if by an apparent waste of film, the director can save time, he will be acting in the best interests of the studio. This is true, providing, of course, that there is no critical shortage of film such as might exist during a war.

TYPES OF PRODUCTION TIME

Production time may be divided into two general types: over-all production time and shooting time. Within shooting time, there is another type we may call actor or talent time.

Certain actors, because of their peculiar talents, demand exceptionally high salaries. These actors may be used in supporting roles and appear in only two or three sequences. It is usually advantageous to schedule those sequences in which the actor works at one time so that the actor may be paid for only a few days rather than for the entire shooting time. This is an example of conserving actor or talent time.

Certain mob sequences require large numbers of extras. In order to conserve talent time, it is usually wise to plan production so as to avoid having those extras on the pay roll except when they are actually working.

PRODUCTION COST SHEET

Date_____

Account_____ Title_____

Footage_____

Work Order Number_____

No.	Classification	Estimated		Actual
		Labor	Mat. & Ser.	
1.	Continuity			
2.	Director			
3.	Assistant Director			
4.	Production Manager			
5.	Cast			
6.	Narrator			
7.	Studio Rental			
8.	Camera Rental			
9.	Sound Channel Rental			
10.	Property Rental			
11.	Wardrobe Rental			
12.	Light Rental, Cable, etc.			
13.	Set Design and Construction			
14.	Set Striking			
15.	Camera Men			
16.	Assistant Camera Men			
17.	Still Camera Men			
18.	Make-up Men			
19.	Stage Crew			
20.	Location Crew			
21.	Trucking			
22.	Location Transportation			
23.	Location Expenses			
24.	Musical Score			
25.	Stock Shots			
26.	Animation			
27.	Titles			
28.	Trick Photography			
29.	Background Stock-D. & P.			
30.	Lavenders			
31.	Projection			
32.	Cutting			
33.	Recording Narrative			
34.	Recording Music			
35.	Recording Effects			
36.	Dubbing			
37.	Negative			
38.	Pos.-Rec.-Direct ft.			
39.	Pos.-Rec.-Nar. ft.			
40.	Pos.-Rec.-Music ft.			
41.	Pos.-Dubbing ft.			
42.	Dev. Negative ft.			
43.	Dev. Sound Track ft			
44.	Ptg. Negative ft			
45.	Ptg. Sound Track ft			
46.	Combined Print ft			
47.	Royalty			
48.	Miscellaneous			
49.	Total Direct Cost			
50.	PRICE			

The budget form used by a small film company. The forms used by the major studios are much more complicated and comprehensive.

METHODS OF SAVING TIME

Before shooting begins, the assistant director prepares a breakdown of the scenario which lists, for each set, the scenes to be shot, the necessary actors, the wardrobe, and the essential props. From this breakdown, the director, the assistant director, and the unit manager prepare a shooting schedule which plans the order in which the sets and locations are to be shot, how long each will take, and the total shooting production time. Thus, the first method of saving time is the preparation of the shooting schedule.

Within the shooting schedule, however, there are many ways in which the director may save time and sometimes cut several days from the schedule.

The first, and perhaps the most important of these, is saving time by example. On the set, the director is the leader, and only if he sets an example can he expect expeditious work from the crew.

The second method of saving time is prior planning. The days when the director could wait until he arrived on the set to have the spirit move and inspire him passed with increased costs and the falling box office. The director must plan, in advance, the scenes he is going to make, the camera angles, and the actions of the actors. Only by knowing these things before shooting can he save the time of the actors and crew during shooting.

By prior planning, the director can take advantage of several rather standard practices. These practices might be called *breaking down the shots, cheating, conservation of set-ups,* and *balancing production factors.* But before he can plan these, he must have a breakdown and a shooting schedule.

THE BREAKDOWN AND SHOOTING SCHEDULE

In the early days, movies were often shot entirely in sequence, that is, scene for scene with the story. Frequently, the crew would leave a set for a day or two only to return to it later because the story continuity returned. Valuable and expensive time

WORKING TITLE: "Closed Case"

SET: Club Royal Entrance (Location)

NUMBER OF SCENES: 9

CAST AND WARDROBE:	SCENE NUMBERS AND DESCRIPTION
Biff Barney Costume A Frank Lundy Costume C Martha Lundy Costume A	51 Long Shot Day Frank Lundy enters club.

	75 Long Shot Day
	      Frank and Martha Lundy drive
	      up in taxi.

EXTRAS AND BITS
Taxi driver
Driver of Barney car
Club Royal Doorman
15 Mixed extras
	76 Close-Up Day
	      Frank Lundy pays fare and
	      CAMERA PANS them to entrance.

	82 Long Shot Day
	      Frank and Martha Lundy leave
	      cafe.

ESSENTIAL PROPS
2 Taxi Cabs
5 Passenger Cars
Submachine gun
	83 Close-Up Day
	      Biff Barney in car. His machine
	      gun ready, he is watching Frank
	      Lundy.

	84 Medium Close-Up Day
	      Frank and Martha walk toward
	      taxi.

EFFECTS
Machine gun effect.
on pavement
	85 Close-Up Day
	      Biff Barney fires submachine
	      gun.

	86 Medium Close-Up Day
	      Frank Lundy is hit and falls to
	      the ground.

CONTRUCTION
Four-section parallel
	87 Long Shot Day
	      As Lundy falls, Biff drives off
	      in car.

SOUND Will work	

A page from a sample Breakdown. The form and information listed in both Breakdown and Shooting Schedule vary widely from studio to studio, some being only a simple form like this, while others also list many factors like costs and rentals. Usually, the crew personnel is listed on the reverse side of the breakdown page.

was wasted in moving back and forth between sets and in carrying actors who had perhaps a few scenes in the beginning of the film and a few scenes at the end. Furthermore, when the shooting was an exterior and if the weather happened to be inclement, costs would roll on and mount while the entire crew and cast sat around waiting for the sun. An extremely costly and wasteful process was the making of a movie!

Today, motion picture production is carefully planned in advance; every move is prearranged; not a minute is spent in unproductive activity. This prior planning normally begins, as far as the director is concerned, with the preparation of the breakdown. Usually prepared by the assistant director or the unit manager, the breakdown lists each set or location, the scenes to be shot on each, the actors and extras required, all essential props, effects, wardrobe, and special construction such as rigging and parallels. From this breakdown, it is possible to estimate the approximate number of shooting days.

The next step is the preparation of a *cross-plot* or *crosshatch*. The crosshatch looks somewhat like a sheet of graph paper. Along the vertical edge are listed all the leads, supporting players, and bits. Along the horizontal edge are listed all the sets and locations. In the appropriate squares are marked the approximate number of days the respective actors work on the set indicated. The assistant director arranges the vertical set strips so that he can group each actor's work into the least possible number of days. He then sees, along the top horizontal edge of his crosshatch, the order in which the sets should be scheduled.

In preparing the shooting schedule, however, there are factors other than talent time to be considered. If the film is being made in a large studio, the assistant director and unit manager must now secure from the production or stage manager the estimated data on studio stage space and construction. Because of the scheduling of other films, it may be desirable and sometimes mandatory that some sets be shot at the beginning of the schedule and others reserved until later.

A Simple CROSS PLOT

A Method of Determining the Schedule

This is what a cross-plot looked like when first laid out from the breakdown.

There was an estimated one day's shooting on each set.

	Living room	Church	Gas station	School room	Golf course	Cafe	Court room
Bill	X		X		X		X
Marty	X			X			X
Mother	X	X		X			X
Judge		X				X	X
Stevens		X	X	X	X	X	X

By juggling the sets, the assistant director saved eleven actor days on the following schedule:
1. Cafe
2. Church
3. Court room
4. Living room
5. School room
6. Golf course
7. Gas station

	Cafe	Church	Court room	Living room	School room	Golf course	Gas station
Bill			X	X		X	X
Marty			X	X	X		
Mother		X	X	X	X		
Judge	X	X	X				
Stevens	X	X	X		X	X	X

Cover sets must be considered. A cover set is merely a stage alternate to an exterior location. If the weather is good on a particular day, the crew will shoot on location. If the weather is bad, the crew works in the cover set on the stage. Each day of contemplated near-by exterior shooting should have several cover sets, if possible, to cover the eventuality of considerable inclement weather. Even on distant locations, cover sets can be provided with the expeditious use of lights, close-ups, and minor interiors.

Some time during the preparation of the shooting schedule, the assistant director goes into conference with the director to find out if he has any particular desires. What sets would the director prefer to shoot first? What sets does he feel he may be able to finish before the estimated time? What sets does he feel may take longer than estimated?

All the essential information is now complete, and the assistant and unit manager balance the factors in preparing the shooting schedule. They try to eliminate any layovers on the part of actors, to provide for sufficient cover sets, to eliminate any unnecessary moves, to mesh their schedule with other studio schedules as far as stage space is concerned, to satisfy the desires of the director, and to make the schedule as short as possible. It's quite a difficult job on some films, and the director must have good reasons if any of his desires make it even more difficult.

BREAKING DOWN THE SHOTS

The layman might expect that the greatest amount of time on the set is spent in rehearsing. This is far from the case. Actually, most time is consumed by the cameraman and his electricians in balancing the lights. Therefore, one of the director's problems is to plan his shots in such a way that this time will be well spent.

The principles involved in saving lighting time are rather simple. The cameraman must change lights or completely relight for each change of camera angle. The greater the change, the more relighting

SHOOTING SCHEDULE

WORKING TITLE: "Closed Case"

NUMBER OF SCENES: 109

DAYS IN SCHEDULE:

2 days Exterior
5 days Interior

DAY AND DATE	SET AND BREAKDOWN PAGE	SCENES	CAST
Mon. June 9	Ext. Lundy Home (1)	5	Frank Lundy Martha Lundy George Policeman
	Ext. Club Royal (5)	9	Biff Barney Frank Lundy Martha Lundy
Tue. June 10	Ext. Court House (9)	3	Biff Barney Martha Lundy George John Dixson
	Ext. Golf Course (3)	8	Frank Lundy John Dixson
Wed. June 11	Int. Lundy Living Room (2)	25	Frank Lundy Martha Lundy George John Dixson Biff Barney Paul Whitely
Thur. June 12 Fri. June 13	Int. Court Room (10)	33	Biff Barney Martha Lundy John Dixson Judge George Paul Whitely Dade Norman Clerk Jury

A page from a sample Shooting Schedule. The first step in the preparation of a schedule is to make a Breakdown of the script. From the Breakdown, a cross plot is prepared, and the schedule is the result of information secured from the cross plot and prevailing studio conditions.

is necessary. Thus, it is the director's job to shoot as many scenes as possible from approximately the same angle. The time that is used in lighting for one shot is allotted to several shots. The director does this by breaking down the individual set-ups on each set and grouping them according to lighting requirements, just as the entire scenario was broken down according to set and cast requirements.

The pattern, generally, is to shoot the long shots first. Then the camera is moved in to get all the closer shots from the angle nearest the long shots. After that, the close shots from another angle are photographed and so on.

While the principle is rather simple, the execution is sometimes difficult. In order to do it, the director must first plan all the set-ups, or shots, and the accompanying action for each sequence. We might call it his editorial or shooting plan. This plan may be mental, it may be in the form of written notes on the edge of the scenario, or it may be in the form of little sketches, pictures, or diagrams. The form depends on the habits and thinking patterns of the individual director. Regardless of how it is done, it is done for but one purpose—to conserve the time spent by the cameraman and his crew in lighting the set.

CHEATING

As discussed in Chapter Two, "The Cut," the background of a scene may or may not have any bearing on the editorial matching of movement or look. This principle is utilized in conserving the lighting time and set construction. For example, in a simple two-walled L set, all four walls may apparently be shown by shooting close-up reverses against the same two walls. The direction of look and movement is cheated with respect to the set, but it remains constant in relation to the camera. New pictures and decorations are substituted in the background walls and the illusion is complete.

By cheating, the director can often make a series of close-ups of many people in a group without ever moving the camera. The actors merely look off the proper side of the camera, and slight but significant changes are made in the background.

In performing such cheats, however, the director must be careful that he doesn't cause the cameraman to take more time. The director must remember the position of the key light for the master scene and not reverse his cheats to such an extent that the cameraman must completely relight. Just as the director must match his action, so must the cameraman match his lighting.

Another method of cheating is the use of the same set for sequences or scenes which, story-wise, take place in entirely different settings. This is accomplished by building one set to handle the requirements of several minor sequences. Then, by using entirely different camera angles, by re-dressing or revamping, the same set is used in place of several sets.

Re-dressing a set merely refers to the changing of props such as furniture, drapes, and pictures.

Revamping a set, a more expensive process, refers to changing physical aspects of the set itself, such as installing different doors, or repainting or repapering the walls.

Not only can cheating on the use of sets save money by saving on the construction of the set, but it can be a substantial time-saving device. It takes time to move the crew from set to set, and the more the director can cut down on such moves, the more time he can save.

CONSERVATION OF SET-UPS

Since most of the time on the set is spent in lighting, it is quite obvious that the fewer set-ups or shots to be lit, the less will be the shooting time. Thus, the director must not shoot needless scenes; he must make every shot count. To do this, of course, he must have a thorough knowledge of editorial principles. He cannot cover the action from every conceivable angle and depend on the editor to pick and choose and discard those scenes which will not cut.

Set-ups may be conserved, too, by the proper staging of each sequence. Master scenes may often be so planned, through the use of movement, that very few additional angles will be needed. Subject and camera movement causes the transitions from medium shot to close-up and back to medium shot. It is in this way that many directors often shoot four or five script scenes in one set-up.

Of course, it takes longer for the cameraman to set up, light, and execute a difficult moving shot than it does to do a simple static shot. However, if it takes less time than it would to take the four or five set-ups it replaces, it is well worth the effort—economically and artistically. The director must balance and evaluate the different factors and decide which method will make the better film and be the least expensive.

BALANCING PRODUCTION FACTORS

The director has a twofold obligation. He must make a film at least as good and as interesting as originally expected, but at the same time he must not spend more in doing it than allotted in the budget. Thus, he is torn between conflicting ambitions—to make it good and to make it cheap. He realizes that with more money and more time, he can always make a better film, but he must know where to stop. The days when a director could forget the budget and concentrate exclusively on making a superepic went out with the British tax and higher costs.

Years ago, a young director was given $20,000 and a two-week schedule to make a film about railroads. He took nine weeks, spent much, much more than the $20,000, and came up with *The Iron Horse*. In 1948, the same director, John Ford, saved $800,000 and cut his schedule from seventy to forty-three days as he filmed *Fort Apache*.

The director must continually weigh artistic niceties against economic necessities. He must first decide what he wants to achieve and then work out a plan for doing it within the limits allowed him. Sometimes he will find that the economic way is also the best way, and then again he will find that accomplishment of his aim is impossible within the budget and schedule allowed him.

He will often find, for example, that within certain limits a faster shooting tempo is conducive to good actor performance. Long delays between scenes and repeated takes sometimes cause an actor to become stale. He loses his continuity of tempo and his spontaneity. On the other hand, repeated takes are sometimes necessary to get just the feel from a scene that the director wants.

Movement is essential to a well-planned picture, but dolly shots, which so often necessarily accompany movement, take time. However, if the master scene is well planned, the director will need only a minimum of cut-ins or cut-aways. Thus, he actually spends less time and less film on the sequence with the result that he gets ahead of his schedule.

Not only must the director balance creative desires against economic realities, but he must continually balance economic realities against each other. Frequently, he must decide whether to stress shooting time or talent time. In a given sequence requiring a large mob but only a few high-paid stars, he knows that he can finish with the mob in two days, but in so doing, he will take four days to finish the sequence. On the other hand, he can retain the mob for three days, but will also finish the sequence in three days. His answer will depend on comparative costs and the type of studio for which he is working. Perhaps his best bet is to turn the two alternatives over to the unit manager and let him decide.

Sometimes the director must balance overshooting against the time factor. At first glance this may appear to be an impossible situation; apparently, overshooting will necessarily increase time. On the contrary, however, there are certain types of sequences in which overshooting can actually save time! One type is a sequence wherein there is considerable dialogue between two or three people but practically no movement. All transitions must be made by means of the cut, and as we cut from close-up of one to close-up of another to a re-establishing medium shot, we repeatedly return to composition and framing seen before. Let's look at an example.

The sequence is of a boy and a girl in a corner booth of a small café. There are five pages of dialogue. We bring them into the booth by means of camera and subject movement, and after they finally get their orders from the waiter, we have these five pages of dialogue with no movement other than their eating and their changes of expression. Neither of them has a long speech, and they both know their dialogue very well.

To cover this sequence, we would need five different angles: a medium two shot from the side, an over-the-shoulder medium close-up of each, and a close-up of each. We know we will need the medium two shot at the beginning, for a speech or two in the middle, and at the end. That makes three scenes from the same set-up. For the other scenes, however, our solution is not so simple. If we shoot just the portions necessary according to the scenario, we will need, let us say, four sections of the dialogue from each of the four angles. In addition, we will need some overlap between each of the scenes so that they may be cut together.

We know from experience that each time we stop the camera there is confusion on the set, and it takes some time to allow the cameraman to make more last-minute adjustments, possibly rehearse, go on the bells, get the stage quiet, and start again. Furthermore, it takes film to get up to speed and slate. Thus, we find that it may be more economical in both time and film if we simply shoot the entire five pages of dialogue completely through for each of the four angles. We may be criticized for waste when the studio executives see the rushes, but we know we have actually saved them money!

Despite the best-laid plans, the director knows that exigencies will arise during shooting that pose entirely new problems. What had been planned as a rather simple moving shot becomes a time-consuming set-up when the sound man and the cameraman can't seem to solve a mike shadow problem. A line becomes a mental block for one of the actors, and on each take he flubs or forgets. He becomes distraught and excited. The director may have to revise his staging and shooting plan.

A retake of a scene shown in the rushes that morning consumes so much time that the director knows he will not finish with certain actors that day as he had planned. The schedule for the next day must be changed, new actor calls sent out, and possibly a conflict with another company working in the same studio may have to be ironed out.

With all his economic problems, the director knows that he may cut a budget to half, but if the completed film is not good enough to make a profit, even that half will be wasted. The final result of his work will be on the screen!

CHAPTER TEN

PEOPLE AND PICTURES

If the preceding chapters have done nothing more, I hope they have impressed upon the reader the value of teamwork and prior planning. All too often a director is handed a scenario and expected to commence shooting almost immediately. Some commercial clients, studio executives, and even producers seem to think that with the completion of their own business arrangements a director should be able to go right into shooting production. On some simple commercial jobs, this may be the case, but if the film has any scope whatsoever, the director has much to do before the cameras can roll.

Just becoming familiar with the scenario is much more than an overnight job. If the film is to be produced at all economically, the director must become as well acquainted with the scenario as are the producer and the writer who may have been working on it for months. The director must study it until he is as familiar with the sequence of events to be portrayed as he is with those in his own life. He must almost memorize it!

After he has become familiar with his scenario, the director must sometimes select locations, cast, and help design the sets. He must plan the exact action and camera set-ups. He must lay out the order in which he will shoot the set-ups, and he must balance all possible production factors so that the film may be produced as economically and artistically as possible. But his planning is only the beginning.

Upon the decisions of the director depends much of the planning of the crew. After he has firmly in mind just how he is going to shoot the film, each key member of the crew must plan his own work so that the production team may function smoothly and efficiently. The cameraman and the sound man must become acquainted with the sets and locations, and they must know the types of angles and actions contemplated by the director. Thus, their plans can only start after his are pretty well jelled. Too, the prop man must secure the many and varied props which will be used in the filming. Costumes must be fitted and sometimes tailored—and this cannot be done until casting is complete. Location arrangements must be made. Crew and actors must be fed and housed. Transportation must be arranged. The efficiency of the most important and most expensive phase of production, the shooting, depends upon the planning that goes before it.

With the completion of shooting, however, the film is far from complete. Although I have not discussed the editing in any detail, it frequently takes longer than all the other phases together. Editing the rough cut, changing, rechanging, and polishing, the preparation of music and sound-effect tracks, special effects, titles, opticals, the processing of the dupe negatives and fine grains needed for the titles and opticals, the dubbing—all these processes take time, and to the finished picture they are just as important as is the shooting phase. Many a well-written and well-directed film has been vitally harmed during the last stages of production.

Sometimes the technicians and artists engaged in these different crafts before, during, and after shooting forget the many others whose work helps make the finished picture. They begin to feel that it is their particular craft, and their craft alone, that carries the completed film. They forget that the finished product reflects the combined efforts of many different crafts and abilities.

BALANCING THE CRAFTS

While the film artist or technician must understand that he is part of a cooperative effort, he cannot himself balance the importance of his work against the work of others. When the efforts of different crafts conflict, it is the director who must make the decision as to their relative importance to the scene in question.

The artist or technician—the sound man, the cameraman, the actor, or the editor—must have a pride and satisfaction in his work that comes only with the feeling that his is the most important work of the production. He must continually strive for perfection. Certainly he will do his job better if he knows the basic problems of the other crafts, but he must continually strive for the highest quality in his own work, regardless of the problems of others. When the physical requirements of his work run afoul of the requirements of others, he must, upholding his standards, try to work out a common solution. If he should finally feel that an impasse has been reached, he should present the problem to the director in the spirit of teamwork that he knows will produce a better film. As far as the director is concerned, which craft is carrying the emphasis in the particular sequence in question?

Almost every day the director must make decisions which prohibit the highest quality, for example, of sound or photography. Only the director knows exactly the effect he wants, and only he can decide which crafts are most important in achieving that effect. At one time it may be sound versus camera, at another camera versus actor, at still another actor versus sound, and at still another sound versus set design.

Perhaps the sequence involves several close-ups which the director desires to be played in depth and to have a certain quality of dramatic perspective. In order to accomplish this it is necessary that the cameraman use a wide angle lens. This, of course, means that the camera will be quite close to the subject and the microphone, and a sound problem arises. The mixer feels that he cannot eliminate the sound of the camera.

Now, to the mixer, the solution seems quite simple; merely place a longer lens on the camera and move it away from the microphone! To do this, however, would defeat everything for which the director is striving. The short depth of field of the longer lens would mean that the scene would be out of focus if played in depth, and the dramatic effect desired from the violent perspective would be lost. Another solution must be found, and whether that solution involves tying blankets around the camera, having the actor speak more loudly, or having inferior sound, the camera perspective must remain.

Another problem may also involve sound and camera. Perhaps a scene, in which there is considerable subject and camera movement, must be played with a confidential or low-level tone of voice. In order to record the dialogue, it is essential that the microphone be quite close to the actors and that the mike placement be held to very close tolerances. However, since the scene involves so much subject and camera movement, lighting is also a problem in that it is quite difficult to avoid mike shadows. In such a case, the director might decide that even though lighting quality might suffer somewhat, the highest quality sound recording is more important than the highest quality lighting.

When technicians are unable to coordinate their conflicting interests, it is the director who must decide as to their relative importance. However, the director cannot be expected to solve the technical problems themselves. He is not a technician. He is, however, a coordinator of technicians, and only he knows the over-all effect desired on the screen. Thus, he should be expected to explain the relative contributions of the crafts involved with respect to the particular effect desired.

In balancing the crafts, there is one mistake the director should never make. He should never allow the desire for mere technical perfection to mar the story, the actions, or the reality of the scene.

It is in that respect that many foreign theatrical films are superior to our own American product.

THEATRICAL FILMS

American theatrical films are as technically perfect as the best technicians in the world can make them. And yet, somehow, many of them fail to attract and hold their audiences. Perhaps part of the cause of this may be that they are produced with too much emphasis on technical perfection at too great a cost to story and reality, but it is more likely that we, the American audience, expect too much from every film.

How many novels published during the course of one year are of really high calibre? On the other hand, how many novels are mere trash, not worthy of the intelligent reader? Can we expect the percentage of really good films to be any better than the percentage of really good books? Books are the creative efforts of single individuals and, as such, have a fairly good opportunity to be honest and sincere. Film scripts, on the other hand, often reflect the inbreeding of Hollywood ideas, the influence of the production moneylender, extreme commercialism—in short, the film factory, involving the combined efforts of several writers, a producer, and a director. As products of such combined efforts, films often lose their individuality and singleness of purpose.

Most critics agree that the fundamental reason for failure of most films lies in the writing—and yet we can be too harsh in our criticism of the writer. Writing for the screen is no longer a job requiring tasteful imagination and a knowledge of screen technique. Writers must conform to budget requirements, the whims of their producers, and the many, many don'ts of the motion picture code. The villain must never be Irish, Jewish, Negro, Italian, Republican, Democrat, Catholic, doctor, or clergyman. In short, unsympathetic characters must be nonentities. Furthermore, "right" must always triumph over "wrong," and the sanctity of the home must never be violated without just retribution. The result of these and many more restrictions is that screen writing can seldom be sincere. True art is always sincere.

How can theatrical motion pictures ever be more than a form of commercial entertainment? Perhaps their audiences don't want them to be more. Nevertheless, in my opinion, just as long as both film producers and the public allow minor pressure groups to dictate requirements for screen stories, just so long will we be afflicted with much of the innocuous tripe that is not even acceptable commercial entertainment. It is indeed a credit to the theatrical film industry that it is able to produce as many fine films as it does. Somehow, some way, it must be given the freedom that is accorded every other art.

It is true that films have a tremendous responsibility in educating our youth, but it is also true that in limiting the scope of screen stories to trivial subjects, we are depriving the mature thought of the country of its just incentive. At least some movies should be an incentive to the mature person! This problem of film censorship by minor pressure groups is indeed a serious one. Certainly I do not know the answer, but I do know that as long as the present condition continues, the true potential of the American film as an informative, educational, and entertainment medium will remain remote. Somehow, the industry and the public must find the answer —be it films classified as to their legal audiences, or be it in the same freedom that is allowed the press or the individual artist or writer.

An important judgment was rendered by the United States Supreme Court in its 1952 decision concerning *The Miracle*, the Italian film banned in New York on grounds of being sacrilegious. In its decision, the court ruled that these grounds were unconstitutional, and for the first time guaranteed films the constitutional protection of freedom of speech. It is still too early to judge the ultimate effects of this ruling, but certainly more test cases will follow. As this book goes to press, controversy is raging over *The Moon Is Blue*, the film version of F. Hugh Herbert's play. With words like "passion" and "seduce" in the dialogue, the film has been turned down by some of the many groups which "judge" American movies.

Another critical failure of theatrical films lies in the method of their presentation to the public. The double feature was born in the depression days of the thirties, and today the industry is still saddled with a practice which it knows alienates many potential customers. Unfortunately, all of many surveys have indicated that the majority of the public, including teen-agers, are in favor of the double feature. At the same time, the minority—the more intelligent and mature section of the populace—is strongly opposed to it. In pleasing one group of people, the industry has repelled another group. The result, of course, has contributed to the falling box office.

If the theatrical motion picture industry is to survive and compete with television, it must solve these problems. If it doesn't solve them, it will become merely the servant of television, and the public motion picture theater will disappear.

ABOUT WIDE SCREEN AND 3D

The present answer of the theatrical film industry to the competition of television is the development of wide screen and three-dimensional films. This trend—revolution might be a better term—started with the New York presentation of *Cinerama* and continued with the development of various forms of wide screen processes, and it was marked by a new emphasis upon three-dimensional films, which were first shown in the early thirties and then abandoned. A short discussion of the various processes might be of interest.

Cinerama, the forerunner of the wide screen, uses a camera with three films, and each of the three 27mm. lenses is set at 48-degree angles to its adjacent lens. The screen used in projection is extremely large and curved, filling the entire viewing angle of the audience, and the three projectors throw synchronized images which overlap slightly in order to form the whole large image. In addition, Cinerama employs multiple loud-speakers and sound tracks in such a way that the audience receives sound effects from the direction from which they should normally come. This principle is the basis of a new development called *Stereophonic Sound*, now used in most wide screen presentations.

The wide screen process most discussed, at present, is *Cinema-Scope*. Developed by 20th Century-Fox, CinemaScope is made possible by a lens invented by M. Henri Chretien of France. The lens, called an anamorphoscope, compresses and distorts an extremely wide angle view onto 35mm. film. Upon projection of the film through a compensating lens, the image is spread horizontally to its original shape. The result is a projected picture 2.55 times as wide as it is high as compared to the conventional 1.37 x 1 proportions. The CinemaScope image fills almost the entire horizontal angle of view of the audience, but it is restricted in height. As a result, the CinemaScope audience has somewhat the illusion of looking through a horizontal slit, and controversy has arisen in the industry as to the most desirable screen proportions. My own feeling is that you can't beat the artistically perfect rectangle wherein the diagonal of a square is equal to the base of a rectangle which maintains the original height of the square. These proportions, also convenient for television, would, however, defeat the purpose for which the wide screen is being developed.

Frequently confused with Cinerama and CinemaScope is the three-dimensional film—sometimes called 3D. Actually, there are very distinct differences. The wide screen processes render only an illusion of depth while 3D is, in fact, stereoscopic. 3D, however, involves the use of polaroid glasses, and it is questionable whether theater audiences will accept their continued use.

The most obvious advantage of the wide screen processes is their adaptability to the presentation of musical comedies and outdoor extravaganzas like *King Kong* and *Gone With the Wind*. However, they lack the intimacy desirable for close, intimate stories like *The Four Poster*.

Because of the sound arrangement and the fact that the image fills the entire viewing angle of the audience, Cinerama renders a remarkable illusion of depth and reality. However, it must be remembered that it is not three-dimensional. Furthermore, audiences object to the vertical lines on the screen where the three images are joined. Another of the disadvantages of Cinerama is the expense involved in its use. The cost of the equipment, about $75,000, is not negligible, and to convert a theater to its use is really a major construction job.

The cost of installing the screen and projection facilities for CinemaScope, on the other hand, is not prohibitive. CinemaScope screen proportions, however, do give the audience an illusion of looking through a horizontal slit, and the wide-angle lens distortion sometimes renders very displeasing effects.

As compared to wide screen, the use of 3D is relatively simple. Its greatest drawback is that the audience must wear glasses, and if one tilts his head too much the image may be scrambled. Furthermore, 3D patrons often complain of eyestrain and headaches which they attribute to technical imperfections which may, in time, be corrected.

Wide screen and 3D are both so new that directorial problems and screen techniques as applied to them have not yet clearly crystallized. However, principles learned in the filming of *The Robe,* the first production in CinemaScope, and the various efforts in 3D are worthy of discussion.

Initial production efforts indicate that 3D screen techniques will differ from conventional "2D" or "flat" techniques, much as solid geometry differs from plane geometry. Directors and cameramen will first have to understand present-day practices and then apply them in terms of space and solids. Of course, some 2D techniques may not apply, but many 2D principles may become even more important. For example, the principle of playing movement toward and away from the camera—rather than at right angles to it—may be not only a desirable, pleasing effect as in 2D, but may become an absolute necessity in 3D. This, however, is not a recommendation for bombarding the audience with flying spears and leaping lions. The objective should be to play the action physically apart from the audience—and in depth behind the screen or "picture window." Although the audience must be captured mentally and emotionally, "placing it bodily" in the midst of physical turmoil can break the spell so necessary to complete emotional subjection.

Wide screen techniques are quite different. At first, with the introduction of Cinerama, it was thought that all the standard techniques—the use of opticals, cuts, close-ups, and movement—would be outmoded. The frame lines of the normal screen are used as definite tools by the director and cameraman, and, without these, the pointed close-up becomes merely a large subject and the exclusion of extraneous matter extremely difficult. In spite of this, however, it was soon learned that many of the standard techniques would still apply in wide screen. But there are, and will be, changes. Present day principles of composition are not too satisfactory in wide screen, and the use of movement and the cut may be somewhat altered. Because of the large screen, the need for cuts will be reduced. When cuts are made, however, the rules for composition and the cut may have to be applied even more rigidly than with conventional film. It will be essential that important subjects be in the same general area of the frame for any two shots which are to be cut together. Furthermore, when cutting from a long shot to a close-up, care must be taken to draw the eye to the area of the long shot frame at which the close-up will be made. This may be done by lighting, staging of the subjects, and by movement. Movement, in wide screen, will be even more useful than in conventional films, and there may be many developments in the art of playing scenes in depth. The techniques of the legitimate stage may be wedded to the movement of the motion picture.

Both 3D and the wide screen processes, in their present stages of development, are—in my opinion—little more than technical innovations designed to draw the public away from television sets and into the theaters. They may be the "shots in the arm" which will recapture the box office, but theatrical film producers, if they are to hold that box office, must sooner or later face the same problem they have been facing with conventional film. As has been proven again and again, good films will make money, regardless of the competition of television and regardless of their method of presentation. Poor films, once the novelty of 3D and wide screen is ended, will not make money. Pertinent themes—imaginative stories—able and honest presentation—these are the requirements of a commercially successful film in today's competition. And no amount of pretty wrapping will long disguise an inferior product!

If wide screen or 3D is universally accepted, the new techniques developed with them will not outmode screen technique as we know it today. The continued growth of television and films for television will simply mean that wide screen and 3D will be new additional crafts. Each craft will survive and develop with the growth of its medium, and most principles will be used interchangeably. It may well be that directors of all visual media— "flatties," television, films for television, 3D, and wide screen—are entering into a great new age of development and of possibilities for development where the old is not discarded—but rather used in itself, combined with the new, and developed into entirely new techniques.

The field of the director still may be in its infancy!

THE BUSINESS FILM

Not nearly as much publicized as the theatrical motion picture industry is the production of business and commercial films. Centered in New York, Detroit, and Chicago, this segment of the industry makes the advertising and good will movies required by American industry. From the television spot commercial to the excellent documentaries presented by some of the larger corporations, the production of business films often presents problems unknown to the theatrical producer. One of these is the omnipotence of the client or account executive.

Inasmuch as the client is paying for the film, it is only natural that he should have definite ideas as to what he wants. Too often,

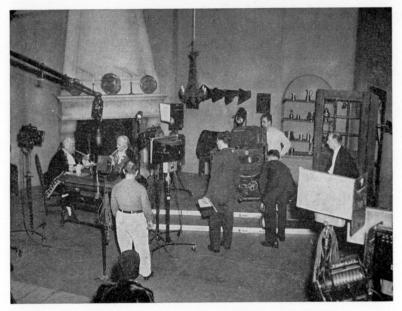

(Courtesy of Audio Productions, Inc.)

Making a commercial film. Hans Mandell directs a scene for *The Search for Security*, produced for the Institute of Life Insurance by Audio Productions, Inc.

however, he tells the producer, writer, and director not only *what* he wants but also *how* he wants it done. And, unacquainted with screen technique and the problems peculiar to film production, the client is often responsible for the poor quality of his own film.

The client who recognizes that film writing and film production are each just as much a business and a specialty as his own particular field is almost certain to secure the best film for his money. Certainly the client would not care to see a screen director take charge of the production line in his plant. By the same token, the screen director knows that the client is not fitted to handle film production. A little knowledge is a dangerous thing, and the amateur who makes 16mm. movies of his family and friends is no more qualified to produce professional films than is the basement tinkerer qualified to direct the production of automobiles. Nor will the casual reading of a book qualify one to produce either films or cars!

It must be admitted, however, that the weakness of some business films is not the fault of the client. While most commercial producers have professionally reliable organizations, there are some who operate on a financial shoestring and have no particular interest in the quality of their work. Indeed, even if they had the interest, they would not have the ability or experience to follow it through.

Thus, the client who would secure a better business film has to do two things: secure an unquestionably reliable producer and keep his own hand out of the production. What he wants, his objectives, he most certainly should insist upon, but how to secure those objectives he should leave to the professional.

THE EDUCATIONAL FILM

One of the constructive outgrowths of World War ll was the impetus given the motion picture as an educational medium. Today the armed forces have a vast library of training films produced both commercially and by the Signal Corps Pictorial Center.

Aside from those produced for the military, many educational films are being produced for school and college distribution. The 1953 edition of *The Educational Film Guide* lists over eleven thousand subjects.

Despite the tremendous growth in production, however, educators and film producers have come to very few really definite conclusions as to the best methods of teaching through films. Unfortunately, surveys on this question have, for the most part, been conducted by individuals apparently ignorant of basic screen techniques. One time I found that a certain organization was spending time, money, and effort on a survey designed to discover the merits of opticals in teaching films! That is like trying to discover the merits

(Courtesy Caravel Films, Inc.)

The problems a commercial film director runs into! In *Jerry Pulls the Strings,* string puppets were played in depth. The film was directed by David Pincus for Caravel Films. It was sponsored by the American Can Company.

of commas, periods, and paragraphs in a textbook. As discussed in the opening chapters of this book, screen techniques have been developed through the years with the adaptation of established principles. Surveying organizations should learn those principles and then conduct studies on questions that the educational film producer is really desirous of knowing.

For a given audience, how many teaching points can logically be included in a film teaching mechanical principles? . . . abstract theories? . . . attitudes? Is narration or dialogue more effective in teaching procedures, attitudes, and principles? How does the number of teaching points vary with the subject matter? What is the maximum length of a good teaching film? How effective is the story-plot approach as opposed to the straight expositional approach? These and many other like questions confront every screen writer and producer when they begin to plan a teaching film. Such questions could profitably be studied by educational research organizations. But let them not waste time in studying fundamentals learned long ago by theatrical film producers. Film is a language which is understood by children and adults alike. Let us try not to change the language but rather to learn how to apply it to the type of film we are making.

Through years of experience in both classroom and film production, I have reached certain tentative conclusions regarding educational films. These conclusions, briefly discussed below, are based only on my individual observations, and they should be interpreted in that light. Some have been substantiated by survey findings; some have not; none, however, to my knowledge, have been invalidated.

It should be recognized that the moving, flickering light of the motion picture screen has, in itself, a certain hypnotic influence. Unless the onlooker is interested enough to overcome this influence, he will be inclined toward sleep. While he may not actually doze, his senses will be dulled and his receptive powers at their weakest. Thus, the educational film must motivate before it can teach.

Motivation, of course, depends upon the audience. A film making no attempt to motivate could be extremely interesting to an audience interested in the subject matter. However, if the audience had no previous interest in the subject matter, the same film could put them to sleep. This factor is all too often unrecognized by the subject-matter experts who act as technical advisers and reviewers. In being themselves interested, they assume that others will be. For example, a dry, expositional approach to military organization might be interesting to the army officer, but from the new inductee it probably would elicit little response. A straightforward presentation of economic principles might find favor with the economics teacher, but to the art student, forced to take economics as a required college course, it might be extremely boring. Thus, before we can decide on the type of motivation, we must decide upon the type of audience for which the film is intended.

One of the most effective methods of motivation is the story-plot format. This was applied quite effectively by the greatest teacher of them all some two thousand years ago. Perhaps best remembered is His parable—and the philosophy—of the Good Samaritan. The story-plot, with certain types of subject-matter for certain audiences, is still just as effective in today's teaching films.

I feel that whenever possible the story-plot format should be used. I do not, however, believe that the gimmick picture, the story used as a vehicle *only*, is of much value. To be valuable, the story must be part of the teaching doctrine.

Suppose we wish to teach salesmanship. The intended audience is the general academic students of college level. What better way than to follow two competing salesmen and get the audience interested in which one is going to win out? We follow an interesting story of competition between two men, and, going right along with the story, a narrator interposes at times and explains the wheres and whys.

Or perhaps we wish to orient soldiers on the procedures of an infantry platoon in the attack. The army spends thousands for maneuvers to teach the same thing. What better way is there on film than to follow an infantry platoon as they attack an enemy stronghold? Here is basic story. Will they or will they not secure the objective? And here the audience lives, through film, the actual procedures we are trying to teach. Such a film was *The Rifle Platoon in The Attack*, written by James Handley and directed by myself.

On the other hand, many subjects do not lend themselves to the story format, and to try to drag in a story merely as a vehicle would, I believe, be an error. In such a case, motivation must be secured in some other manner. I remember one such film, a British production, which I saw during World War II. Called *Booby Traps*, it covered different isolated points, and to combine them into one single story would have resulted in a highly illogical situation. However, the film had excellent motivation. The visual presentation showed many little vignettes of life concerning booby traps. The motivating force was the extremely clever narration, fraught with dry humor that most soldiers found quite funny. In awaiting the next humorous crack, few in the audience missed the teaching points.

Two of the greatest failures in our educational films are verbose narration and the inclusion of too much subject matter. In attempting to stretch a limited budget over considerable material, educators often force the film producer to lose the value of what is actually spent. Only a few major points should be taught in each film, and the audience should have sufficient time to digest each point. The inclusion of too much material, with fact piled upon fact, results only in confusion, for, unlike the textbook or the lecture, the film cannot be interrupted by questions of the student.

Including too much subject matter happens more frequently when narration is being used than when dialogue is the audio vehicle. Explanations with narration are direct and quick, and it is very easy for the film maker to include too many facts too quickly. Upon viewing such a film, the student becomes confused and learns little. When dialogue is the method of presentation, the film maker is forced to allow time for verbal interplay, gestures, and bits of business. As a result, the student is given a chance to think and to digest the material presented. Of course, the use of dialogue is almost impossible when dealing with certain types of subject matter, and narration can be extremely effective *if properly used.* Perhaps the best method, in many types of films, is a combination of both narration and dialogue; narration to point up and explain the major teaching points, dialogue to amplify the points, motivate, and allow the audience time to think and to compare.

One factor which is sometimes forgotten by the educational film producer is the importance of the visual presentation. As mentioned earlier, the newsreel-type film places the emphasis on the narration or audio, while the continuity-type presentation places the emphasis on the visual. We know that the human being remembers more of what he sees than of what he hears. Therefore, it follows that the continuity-type film should be more effective for teaching. In line with this way of thinking, one European country makes only silent teaching films and forces the producer and educator to think only in visual terms.

The role of the director in the production of an educational film is perhaps even more important than in other types of films. Conditioned by Hollywood theatrical films, the public has learned to expect technical perfection. By "perfection" I do not mean the use of trick wipes and dissolves to cover the lack of film continuity, but rather a simple, smooth, visual presentation that results from thoughtful writing and expert direction. The educational film must conform to that standard. If it does not, the presentation will be amateurish and its authenticity weak.

ABOUT TELEVISION

Although there has been a merger between a major Hollywood studio and a radio broadcasting chain, and although a very successful experiment in phonovision has been conducted in Chicago, the effect of television upon the motion picture industry has not yet crystallized. The use of films for television has become more frequent, and television engineers have found ways to telecast film in a picture quality approaching the clarity of the live show. In addition, those engineers are even finding ways of placing the picture on tape just as sound is now put on tape. What this holds for the future is difficult to predict.

Unfortunately for the live television show, many television directors have still not progressed as far as their technical cohorts. It is true that many of them have learned much about screen technique, and that an influx of picture-trained people is gradually raising directorial quality. It is also true that some of the live shows have achieved an artistic and technical standard which was deemed impossible a few years ago. In spite of this, however, some television directors still insist upon dissolving from medium shot to close-up and in shooting false reverses, and some cameramen still have little compositional appreciation. Many fine actors, improperly handled by directors with only stage experience, still project to a theoretical balcony when the camera and microphone are only a few feet away. These failings, of course, can and will be corrected in time, but, on the other hand, other failures of the live show are quite difficult to correct because of the very nature of television production.

The live television show is usually produced by means of three, or possibly four, cameras. The show is played in continuity, like a stage play, and the cameras are moved about for their different angles. The director, at the console and watching the monitoring screens of the different cameras, indicates to the technical director when which cameras are to be telecast. Naturally, each camera must stay out of the field of the other cameras, and as a result angles are often awkward and cutting sometimes rough. Furthermore, it is next to impossible for the cameraman to light properly for more than one camera. As a result of these difficulties, many competent television directors use subject and camera movement almost exclusively and stage their scenes in depth. While this is a perfectly good technique, it can be and is being overdone. For certain effects, playing a scene in depth is very effective, but when the technique is used merely to surmount production difficulties, it can become tiring and quite inappropriate to the mood of the sequence.

The solutions lie in the future!

TEMPERAMENT

Publicity agents, magazine writers, and columnists would sometimes have the public believe that a film studio is a temperamental tempest, full of screaming directors and turbulent actors. Actually, agents, writers, and columnists have written and said much more about the temperament of artists and performers than exists in fact. On the sets of the most competent and best known directors, temperament is a thing seldom known. Competent people have no time for childish displays of temper. There is a job to be done. The truly great do not indulge in juvenile tantrums, and they permit no such antics on the part of those who work with them.

Usually it is the third-rate director, actor, or cameraman who rants and raves to cover his own incompetence—or to win an argument through emotion rather than reason.

In some few cases the weakness of really great artists seems to be an inability to control their emotions. However, could they master themselves I have no doubt that they would gain an even greater command of their art. The director's method of coping with them lies within himself and his own particular personality. Unfortunately, they cannot always be treated as one might treat a dearly loved, but extremely naughty, child.

Temperamental displays disrupt the working efficiency of the crew, distract the cast, and generally make the filming of the story more difficult. Most artists, whether they are in front of or behind the camera, realize this, and if only for the sake of the film of which they are a part, make themselves extremely desirable working companions. Indeed, the higher one looks the less apt one is to find that disagreeable thing called temperament. Some of the finest and greatest people in the business, while certainly very definite as to what they want, are wonderful troupers and open to suggestion from the humblest stagehand.

A DIRECTOR'S GRIPE

Sometimes the public, and even some few production crew members, forget that the film director is quite a normal fellow with his own share of sometimes childish likes and dislikes. For example, even at the risk of appearing to take a somewhat naive approach, I feel compelled to include in this book a few of my own pet gripes.

Number one of my antipathies is the frustrated actor. He is the character who failed completely in front of the camera—or perhaps he never tried—and who now spends his time acting in the projection room, the front office, or the conference room. He is the guy who wows them from his darkened seat in the projection room as the rushes are being shown. He is the guy, too, who gains his point in a conference, not by reasoning, but by his overample histrionics. And he is the guy who is forever invading the front office to tell about things he should be doing.

Another of my pet gripes is the self-appointed detective of the studio. He never wrote, directed, or photographed a scene in his life, but he is a whiz-bang at finding errors in the work of others. Of course, he never approaches the criminal who commits the flaws. Rather, he makes frequent unrequested reports to the front office, so that his discriminative powers may be duly observed.

Less discomforting, but probably more insidious, is the eternal "yes man." He is the director's, the producer's, or the executive's echo, and like an echo, he never has an idea of his own. Surrounded by enough of these characters, even the best directors may soon find themselves slipping.

Motion picture production is a cooperative effort, and there is little room for the unproductive leech. Be he frustrated actor, self-appointed detective, or yes man, the producer who keeps him on the pay roll is headed for destruction. On the other hand, many a sin may be forgiven the worker who really contributes, and we who make films must recognize that creative ability sometimes takes many forms.

A LAST WORD

Like all expositional works, this book contains facts, principles, and opinions. For example, the existence of the Central Casting Corporation and of the different types of producing organizations are facts which cannot be disputed. The rules concerning the cut are principles which have been developed through years of film-making. My opinions regarding type casting and the educational film, for example, are theories based on my own personal experience.

The reader can accept the facts as existing situations which must be dealt with. The principles he should learn as guides to good film-making. Usually they should be followed, but many times they may be disregarded to good effect. However, only the person who understands them is competent enough to disregard them.

Concerning my opinions, they accord with those of many directors and competent film-makers, but they are disputed by others just as competent. For these views I offer no apologies nor further explanation. They have developed through years of directing, and I hope they will continue to develop and change. I offer them merely as the way of thinking of one director.

However, I do wish to comment on my philosophy that a film can live. Frequently, I have referred to a "living scene," or a "living film." How often has a director worked with a difficult scene until he has memorized every line of dialogue, all the gestures of the actors, and each movement of the camera? Certainly, it would seem that the director could see no "life" in such a scene. And yet—on one of the takes—perhaps the first—perhaps the fifth—magic seems to strike the entire set. Suddenly, the director forgets the part he played in planning the scene. He forgets to watch for timing and emphasis. Techniques vanish, and in their place is seen that which is real. The thing is alive! The director—the entire cast and crew—believe it! It lives! I have had that magic strike scenes which I was directing—so much so that tears have clouded my eyes. Most directors have had similar experiences—times when their actors really experienced those emotions which they were expressing. When there are enough scenes like that in a well-constructed and well-written film, who can deny that the film comes to life? I think it does.

From some directors who have read this manuscript I have had a rather curious reaction. I was roundly berated for disclosing trade secrets upon which the profession has been built. To me, that accusation seems naive. There are no "trade secrets"; there are only basic principles, creative minds, and human emotions. Can a mere knowledge of principles create a film?

Can mere words concerning a visual and auditory medium explain how anyone can make use of the principles? No more than a book can teach one to paint or compose a musical score. The written word can only develop or increase an awareness and discuss limited problems. By so doing, those words can ease the task of the screen director in that the readers may become more aware of his problems.

In this book I have tried to present little more than basic directorial knowledge. Many principles which become a little involved I have not even mentioned. I have made only a limited effort to discuss that elusive thing called "art," and I have made no attempt to define the merits of a good or a bad story—even though the story is all-important to the director's success. In short, I have tried to do little more than expose some of the mechanical fundamentals. What, then, you may ask, do I expect the book to accomplish?

This book can, and I hope it will, contribute to a mutual understanding of one another's problems by the writer, the editor, the actor, the cameraman, and the sound man. To the individual who has had no opportunity to learn the language of the film, it can reveal principles and techniques which will make him a better critic of those films he sees; and to the young adult who hopes to enter some phase of professional film production, it can provide a foundation of basic information. But—and this is important—it can never teach anyone to direct motion pictures!

What does make a successful film director? Knowledge of the principles and techniques of motion pictures—understanding of people—ability to sell—innate leadership—love of the dramatic coupled with good taste and imagination. But it takes more than these. The film director must realize that a purely mechanical knowledge of principles and techniques is not enough to create a living motion picture. Most important of all is heart. It is this which brings a film to life.

RELATED BIBLIOGRAPHY

Alton, John, *Painting with Light*. New York: The Macmillan Co., 1950. (A leading Hollywood cameraman discusses lighting.)

Benoit-Levy, Jean, *The Art of the Motion Picture*. New York: Coward-McCann, Inc., 1946. (A discourse on film-making by a leading French director.)

Eisenstein, Sergei M., *The Film Sense*. New York: Harcourt, Brace and Company, 1947. (An intellectual discourse on theory.)

Gaskill and Englander, *Pictorial Continuity*. New York: Duell, Sloan and Pearce, Inc., 1947. (A book for the amateur but which has more of practical value than do many books for the professional.)

Herman, Lewis, *A Practical Manual of Screen Playwriting*. Cleveland: The World Publ. Co., 1952. (To my knowledge, the only practical and complete book on scenario-writing.)

Manvell, Roger, *Film*. London: Penguin Books, Inc., 1950. (Historical and current fact and opinion by a leading British critic.)

Ross, Lillian, *Picture*. New York: Rinehart & Co., Inc., 1952. (The story of the production of *The Red Badge of Courage*, it is more of a novel of the people of Hollywood.)

Smith, Albert E., *Two Reels and a Crank*. New York: Doubleday & Co., Inc., 1952. (Autobiography of the former president of the old Vitagraph studios.)

Spottiswoode, Raymond, *A Grammar of the Film*. London: Faber and Faber, 1935. (An academic study of film technique.)

Spottiswoode, Raymond, *Film and its Technique*. Los Angeles: University of California Press, 1952. (The technical aspects of film production.)

INDEX

205